AMERICAN PICTURE SHOW

A Cultural Reader

AMERICAN PICTURE SHOW

A Cultural Reader

Elizabeth A. Mejia

Maida Kennedy Xiao

Lucyna Pasternak

WASHINGTON STATE UNIVERSITY

PRENTICE HALL REGENTS
Englewood Cliffs, New Jersey 07632

Library of Congress Cataloging-in-Publication Data
Mejia, Elizabeth A., (date)
American picture show : a cultural reader / Elizabeth A. Mejia.
Maida Kennedy Xiao / Lucyna Pasternak.
    p. cm.
Includes bibliographical references.ISBN 0–13–029687–2
1. English language—Textbooks for foreign speakers. 2. United
States—Civilization—Problems, exercises, etc. 3. Motion pictures—
Problems, exercises, etc. 4. Readers—Motion pictures.
5. Readers—United States. I. Kennedy Xiao, Maida, (date).
II. Pasternak, Lucyna. III. Title.
PE1128.M377   1992
428.6′4—dc20   91–4043
                                                             CIP

Acquisitions Editor: **Anne Riddick**
Production Editor: **Shirley Hinkamp**
Copy Editor: **Anne Graydon**
Prepress Buyer: **Ray Keating**
Manufacturing Buyer: **Lori Bulwin**
Scheduler: **Leslie Coward**
Cover Designer: **Jayne Conte**

 © 1992 by Prentice Hall Regents
Prentice-Hall, Inc.
A Division of Simon & Schuster
Englewood Cliffs, New Jersey 07632

Printed in the United States of America
10 9 8 7

ISBN 0-13-029687-2

Prentice-Hall International (UK) Limited, *London*
Prentice-Hall of Australia Pty. Limited, *Sydney*
Prentice-Hall Canada Inc., *Toronto*
Prentice-Hall Hispanoamericana, S.A., *Mexico*
Prentice-Hall of India Private Limited, *New Delhi*
Prentice-Hall of Japan, Inc., *Tokyo*
Simon & Schuster Asia Pte. Ltd., *Singapore*
Editora Prentice-Hall do Brasil, Ltda., *Rio de Janeiro*

Acknowledgements

I would like to thank my parents, Thomas and Mathilde Kennedy and my daughter Pamela Mejia. This manuscript would not have been possible without the extremely patient, hard-working secretarial support of Mrs. Sue Collinsworth.

Elizabeth Mejia
Pullman, Washington
1991

CONTENTS

USING LIBRARY INDEXES   **215**

PREFACE

About the Book

This is an advanced-level, content-based, cultural reader designed for use with classes of ESL students who are preparing to enter American colleges and universities. It is based on the premise that such students must learn *in* English as well as *about* English. In other words, the manipulation of linguistic skills is not enough. Students must learn how to use those skills to generate language and acquire knowledge. The only way to acquire knowledge in a second language is to practice using linguistic skills on content-rich material. It is on this premise that *American Picture Show* is based.

The Structure of the Book

Each chapter of this book—with the exception of the first and the last—is based on a popular American movie. Comprehension of the movie is facilitated by means of several prereadings that explore cultural themes found in the movie. The movie itself is developed by means of a summary and discussion questions. Following the movie unit in each chapter are two movie reviews, one favorable and one critical, for further reading practice. At the end of each chapter are writing exercises by which the students can practice integrating the content that they have learned.

The structure of the chapters simulates the structure by which material is often learned in formal academic settings. First, material is read in a textbook. Then, students often hear a lecture on the material. Finally, students are expected to discuss, read further about, and write about what they have learned. Each part of the chapter serves to build a schema for the next part. The movie prereadings prepare the student to understand the movie. The movie preteaching units prepare the student to understand the movie and discuss it afterwards. The movie itself and the discussion questions about the movie facilitate comprehension of the critical reviews following the viewing of the movie.

Not only the structure but the content of the material is postsecondary level. Articles and reading excerpts are taken from university-level textbooks, newspapers such as the *Los Angeles Times*, and magazines such as *Newsweek, Time*, and *U.S. News & World Report*. All the topics in this book are examinations of American culture. The book provides a multimedia approach to American Studies for ESL students, and much of the material has been classroom tested in such courses.

Hints for Successful Use of This Book

The chapters in this book are not sequential, although it is highly recommended that the first chapter, which details a method for reading advanced-level texts, be covered before undertaking the other chapters. In addition, it should be noted that many of the reading exercises require the student to engage with the text at a very high level of the learning continuum.

Many of the questions require the student to infer and to speculate based on knowledge acquired from previous readings or the movie. Successful use of this book requires a teacher who is willing to accept that there may be more than one correct answer to a question and that credit should be given as much for the way students arrive at an answer as for the answers they develop.

Using the Movies in This Book

Finally, persons using this book may have questions about how best to use the movies in each chapter. The Copyright Law of the United States limits the ways that movies can be used, even in educational settings, but there are a number of useful alternatives available to teachers and students.

One way is to make a class field trip to a cinema to view the movie as part of the theater audience. A second way is to show the movie under the auspices of an instructional media center that has secured the rights to show the movies to large groups of students. Many schools and districts have license agreements with such licensors as Coronet/MTI Film & Video, or offices which can coordinate obtaining appropriate licenses. Third, students may themselves rent copies of a film for at-home viewing. This will give them the opportunity to watch the movie in private surroundings with a group of friends, rewinding and fast forwarding as needed.

The authors of this book would like to state that they only endorse legal methods of showing movies and they encourage all persons using this book to investigate the legal ways to show movies in educational settings.

THE READING CHAPTER

One common misbelief that many students have about reading in English is that it is done by reading in certain directions: left to right, top to bottom, front to back. In other words, when a reader opens a book to read, he starts at the front of the book, at the top of the page, at the left margin, and continues left to right, down the page, to the back of the book, as illustrated in this passage from "Paradox and Dream" by John Steinbeck.

> **Begin here** One of the generalities most often noted about Americans is that we are a restless, a dissatisfied, a searching people. We bridle and buck under failure, and we go mad with dissatisfaction in the face of success. We spend our time searching for security, and hate it when we get it. For the most part we are an intemperate people: we eat too much when we can, drink too much, indulge our senses too much. Even in our so-called virtues we are intemperate: a teetotaler is not content not to drink—he must stop all the drinking in the world; a vegetarian among us would outlaw the eating of meat. We work too hard, and many die under the strain; and then to make up for that we play with a violence as suicidal.
> **End here.**

Such a pattern is sometimes used, but usually by readers who are very familiar with the subject and the language of the reading material. For example, a graduate student in American Studies could probably pick up this passage and read it following this pattern. For such a student, the passage would be quite easy.

However, a college freshman could not expect to pick up this text and understand much by following the pattern. For a freshman, the text would be difficult. It would discuss subjects with which she is unfamiliar, using terms she doesn't know.

The pattern such a student would follow to understand the text would be completely different. She might start at the top of the page on the left, but soon she would come to a word she didn't know. At that point, she would probably glance back at the information she had read before the word to get help to determine the meaning of the word. If she didn't find an answer, she might read on, looking for more help to determine the meaning of the word. Once she felt as though she understood the word, she might even reread the entire passage again. Diagrammatically, the pattern might look like this:

> **Begin here** One of the generalities most often noted about Americans is that we are a restless, a dissatisfied, a searching people. We bridle and buck under failure, and we go mad with dissatisfaction in the face of success. We spend our time searching for security, and hate it when we get it. For the most part we are an intemperate people: we eat too much when we can, drink too much, indulge our senses too much. Even in our so-called virtues we are intemperate: a teetotaler is not content not to drink—he must stop all the drinking in the world; a vegetarian among us would outlaw the eating of meat. We work too hard, and many die under the strain; and then to make up for that we play with a violence as suicidal.
> **End here.**

That is the way a good reader would read a difficult, unfamiliar text. A poor reader might stop at each unfamiliar word and look it up in the dictionary before continuing to read. This would take a lot of time, and by the time the reader finished the page, she probably wouldn't remember what she had read. She might have to reread it two or three times just to understand it.

You can learn to be a good reader of difficult and unfamiliar texts. It takes practice, and at first it may seem slow, but it is worth learning if you want to succeed in college reading.

To start practicing this good reading style, all you need is a text and a pencil and an eraser. As you arrive at unfamiliar words, glance back one or two sentences. If that doesn't help, keep reading. If you are still confused, go back to the unfamiliar word or words and underline them. Then keep reading. Repeat this process until you arrive at the end of the passage. Then, read the whole passage again. As you reread it, you will probably be able to guess the meanings of words you underlined the first time. Erase the lines under any words you now understand. After you have done this, look up any remaining underlined words before turning the page.

Here is an example of the same paragraph with the words the reader underlined during the first reading:

> One of the generalities most often noted about Americans is that we are a restless, a dissatisfied, a searching people. We bridle and buck under failure, and we go mad with dissatisfaction in the face of success. We spend our time searching for security, and hate it when we get it. For the most part we are an intemperate people: we eat too much when we can, drink too much, indulge our senses too much. Even in our so-called virtues we are intemperate: a tee-totaler is not content not to drink—he must stop all the drinking in the world; a vegetarian among us would outlaw the eating of meat. We work too hard, and many die under the strain; and then to make up for that we play with a violence as suicidal.

Here is the same passage after the second reading. Notice how much has been erased:

> One of the generalities most often noted about Americans is that we are a restless, a dissatisfied, a searching people. We bridle and buck under failure, and we go mad with dissatisfaction in the face of success. We spend our time searching for security, and hate it when we get it. For the most part we are an intemperate people: we eat too much when we can, drink too much, indulge our senses too much. Even in our so-called virtues we are intemperate: a tee-totaler is not content not to drink—he must stop all the drinking in the world; a vegetarian among us would outlaw the eating of meat. We work too hard, and many die under the strain; and then to make up for that we play with a violence as suicidal.

The reader who marked this page explained her reasons for erasing the underlined words as follows:

1. "Restless" is in a list of words with "dissatisfied" and "searching." It probably means something like those two words.

2. "Intemperate" means people who eat and drink too much. The colon (:) shows where examples of the meaning start.

3. "Virtues" are to be a teetotaler or a vegetarian. The colon (:) shows where examples of the meaning start.

4. "A teetotaler" doesn't drink. An intemperate teetotaler doesn't believe anyone should drink.

5. "A vegetarian" is mentioned after teetotaler. It must be an example of someone who doesn't do something, like a teetotaler; not drinking. A vegetarian probably doesn't eat meat.

6. "Outlaw" means to be an intemperate vegetarian. Maybe it is someone who is very serious about not eating meat.

After two readings, you can look up the remaining words in a dictionary. However, *a* "dictionary" does not mean just any dictionary. Some dictionaries are definitely better than others.

Bilingual dictionaries are not a good way to learn new vocabulary words. Some of the most common problems with bilingual dictionaries are out-of-date linguistic information and imprecisely defined words. Another problem is that such dictionaries encourage you to learn in translation. If you plan to attend an American or Canadian university, you will need to know how to learn new ideas, concepts, and terms *in English*.

There are several good American English dictionaries that you might want to consider. However, since you will probably be doing most of your reading outside of class, spend the extra money to buy a collegiate dictionary and a pocket dictionary. You can carry the pocket dictionary with you when you are away from home and keep the collegiate dictionary for use at home.

Assume you want to locate the meaning of the word "bridle." The first important clue to look for is the part of speech. In this sentence, "bridle" is used as a verb.

²**bridle** *vb* **bri·dled; bri·dling** \'brid-liŋ, -'l-iŋ\ *vt* **1** : to put a bridle on **2** : to restrain, check, or control with or as if with a bridle; *esp* : to get and keep under restraint (you must learn to ∼ your tongue) ∼ *vi* : to show hostility or resentment (as to an affront to one's pride or dignity) esp. by drawing back the head and chin **syn** **1** see RESTRAIN *ant* vent **2** see STRUT

bri·dle (brĭd'l) *n.* [< OE. *bregdan*, to pull] **1.** a head harness for guiding a horse **2.** anything that controls or restrains —*vt.* **-dled, -dling 1.** to put a bridle on **2.** to curb or control —*vi.* to draw one's head back as an expression of anger, scorn, etc.   BRIDLE

Webster's Ninth New Collegiate Dictionary*   *Webster's New World Dictionary***

*By permission. From Webster's Ninth New Collegiate Dictionary. © 1991 by Merriam Webster, Inc., publisher of the Merriam Webster® dictionaries.
**From the book, Webster's New World Dictionary, Third College Edition. © 1988, used by permission of the publisher, Webster's New World Dictionaries/A division of Simon & Schuster, New York.

In the Webster's Collegiate dictionary there are a total of three definitions listed for "bridle" when it is used as a verb: two transitive (*vt*) uses and one intransitive (*vi*) use. There are also two synonyms given: "restrain" and "strut." An antonym is given for "restrain": "vent." The Webster's pocket dictionary lists two transitive definitions of the verb, one intransitive definition and no synonyms. The sentence uses "bridle" as an intransitive verb. It is followed not by a direct object, but by a prepositional phrase. Therefore, it would be best to look for the meaning of "bridle" under the intransitive verbs. Picking the correct definition becomes a matter of trying out each definition in a restatement of the original sentence to see which definition makes the most sense in the context of the passage. The best restatement for this sentence, given that the author has already said that Americans are a dissatisfied people, would probably be "Americans resent failure."

Sometimes, however, the dictionary can be confusing for foreign students. Often, students will complain that they can't understand the definitions in a dictionary. At first, it may require looking up one of the words used in the definition. This may seem like a long and laborious process, but consider that with each word you look up, you are learning how Americans use and define the word. For example, suppose that the student didn't understand the defining words "show hostility." A good rule would be to check for the meaning of a phrase under the least common word, which in this case would be the word "hostility."

hos·til·i·ty \hä-'stil-ət-ē\ *n, pl* **-ties**   **1 a** : a hostile state   **b** (1) : hostile action   (2) *pl* : overt acts of warfare : WAR   **2** : antagonism, opposition, or resistance in thought or principle   *syn* see ENMITY

*Webster's Ninth New Collegiate Dictionary**

hos·til·i·ty (häs til′ə tē) *n.*, *pl.* **-ties** 1. a feeling of enmity, ill will, etc. **2.** *a)* a hostile act   *b)* [*pl.*] warfare

*Webster's New World Dictionary***

*By permission. From Webster's Ninth New Collegiate Dictionary. © 1991 by Merriam Webster, Inc., publisher of the Merriam Webster® dictionaries.
**From the book, Webster's New World Dictionary, Third College Edition. © 1988, used by permission of the publisher, Webster's New World Dictionaries/A division of Simon & Schuster, New York.

Again, notice the difference in the information in the Webster's Collegiate and the Webster's pocket dictionaries. The Webster's Collegiate lists two major definitions of "hostility." The first definition has two subdefinitions **(1&2).** The first subdefinition is further divided into two subdefinitions **(a&b).** Subdefinition **b** is divided again into (1) and (2), the last of which has a synonym: "war." In addition a synonym, "enmity," is given for "hostility." The Webster's pocket dictionary lists two definitions, of which (2) is divided into two subdefinitions. No synonyms are given. It makes sense to say "Americans resist/oppose failure," so this would be a good definition of "bridle."

You can use this dictionary technique to learn the meanings of idioms in English. Idioms are particularly difficult for foreign students because the individual words are clear, but the combined meanings are not. Consider the following example:

Mr. Collins is *under the weather* and won't be in today.

"Under" is clear; "weather" is clear. Combined, they make no sense. How is it logically possible to be "under the weather?" This is one clue that you are looking at an idiom. An idiom is a group of words that often have simple, clear, individual meanings, but which usually do not make sense when considered together. The simplest way to determine the meaning of such an idiom is to look for it under the least common words in the dictionary. Nouns and verbs are less common than prepositions, so in this case, you would look for this meaning under the word "weather." As you can see from the following entries, "under the weather" means "ill or drunk."

¹**weath·er** \'weth-ər\ n [ME weder, fr. OE; akin to OHG wetar weather, OSlav vetrŭ wind] **1 :** state of the atmosphere with respect to heat or cold, wetness or dryness, calm or storm, clearness or cloudiness **2 :** state of life or fortune **3 :** disagreeable atmospheric conditions: as **a :** RAIN, STORM **b :** cold air with dampness **4 :** WEATHERING — **under the weather 1 :** ILL **2 :** DRUNK

weath·er (we th'ər) n. [OE. weder] **1.** the condition of the atmosphere with regard to temperature, moisture, etc. **2.** storm, rain, etc. —vt. **1.** to expose to the action of weather **2.** to pass through safely (to weather a storm) **3.** Naut. to pass to the windward of —vi. to become discolored, worn, etc. by exposure to the weather —**under the weather** [Colloq.] ill

Webster's Ninth New Collegiate Dictionary***   *Webster's New World Dictionary*****

A common vocabulary-building technique of language students is to write each new word they look up in a dictionary or thesaurus in a word book. There are several reasons why this is not a good idea for improving college-level reading. First, students usually write the definitions in their native language, thus returning to the idea of learning in translation. Second, writing word books takes valuable time away from reading. Third, many of the words they look up are not high-frequency words. That is, they are words the student only needs once.

What then is the best way to learn the new words you look up? One good way is to put a pencil dot next to any word you look up in a dictionary or thesaurus. If you find yourself looking up a word twice, put another dot next to the word. Any word you need to look up twice is probably a good word to memorize, since it is a high-frequency word in your vocabulary.

Directions: Before you start reading the chapters in this book, practice this reading method on the following passage. Follow these steps: (1) Read the entire passage once. Underline any words you don't understand. (2) Reread the passage two times, erasing any words you have figured out. (3) Look up any remaining words in an English-English dictionary. (4) Discuss the passage and how you made your "guesses" with a small group of your classmates.

PARADOX AND DREAM

John Steinbeck

One of the generalities most often noted about Americans is that we are a restless, a dissatisfied, a searching people. We bridle and buck under failure, and we go mad with dissatisfaction in the face of success. We spend our time searching for security, and hate it when we get it. For the most part we are an intemperate people: we eat too much when we can, drink too much, indulge our senses too much. Even in our so-called virtues we are intemperate: a teetotaler is not content not to drink—he must stop all the drinking in the world; a vegetarian among us would outlaw the eating of meat. We work too hard, and many die under the strain; and then to make up for that we play with a violence as suicidal.

The result is that we seem to be in a state of turmoil all the time, both physically and mentally. We are able to believe that our goverment is weak, stupid, overbearing, dishonest, and inefficient, and at the same time we are deeply convinced that it's the best government in the world, and we would like to impose it upon everyone else. We speak of the American Way of Life as though it involved the ground rules for the governance of heaven. A man hungry and unemployed through his own stupidity and that of others, a man beaten by a brutal policeman, a woman forced into prostitution by her own laziness, high prices, availability, and despair—all bow with reverence toward the American Way of Life, although each one would look puzzled and angry if he were asked to define it. We scramble and scrabble up the stony path toward the pot of gold we have taken to mean security. We trample friends, relatives, and strangers who get in the way of our achieving it; and once we get it, we shower it on psychoanalysts to try to find out why we are unhappy, and finally—if we have enough of the gold—we contribute it back to the nation in the form of foundations and charities.

We fight our way in, and try to buy our way out. We are alert, curious, hopeful, and we take more drugs designed to make us unaware than any other people. We are self-reliant and at the same time completely dependent. We are aggressive, and defenseless. Americans overindulge their children and do not like them; the children in turn are overly dependent and full of hate for their parents. We are complacent in our possessions, in our houses, in our education; but it is hard to find a man or woman who does not want something better for the next generation. Americans are remarkably kind and hospitable and open with both guests and strangers; and yet they will make a wide circle around the man dying on the pavement. Fortunes are spent getting cats out of trees and dogs out of sewer pipes; but a girl screaming for help in the street draws only slammed doors, closed windows, and silence.

Now there is a set of generalities for you, each one of them canceled out by another generality. Americans seem to live and breathe and function by paradox; but in nothing are we so paradoxical as in our passionate belief in our own myths. We truly believe ourselves to be natural-born mechanics and do-it-yourself-ers. We spend our lives in motor cars, yet most of us—a great many of us at least—do not know enough about a car to look in the gas tank when the motor fails. Our lives as we live them would not function without electricity, but it is a rare man or woman who, when the power goes off, knows how to look for a burned-out fuse and replace it. We believe implicitly that we are the heirs of the pioneers; that we have inherited self-sufficiency and the ability to take care of ourselves, particularly in relation to nature. There isn't a man among us in ten thousand who knows how to butcher a cow or a pig and cut it up for eating, let alone a wild animal. By natural endowment, we are great rifle shots and great hunters—but when hunting season opens there is a slaughter of farm animals and humans by men and women who couldn't hit a real target if they could see it. Americans treasure the knowledge that they live close to nature, but fewer and fewer farmers feed more and more people; and as soon as we can afford to, we eat out of cans, buy frozen TV dinners, and haunt the delicatessens. Affluence means moving to the suburbs, but the American suburbanite sees, if anything, less of the country than the city apartment dweller with his window boxes and his African violets carefully tended under lights. In no country are more seeds and plants and equipment purchased, and less vegetables and flowers raised.

Sometimes we seem to be a nation of public puritans and private profligates. There surely can be no excesses like those committed by good family men away from home at a convention. We believe in the manliness of our men and the womanliness of our women, but we go to extremes of expense and discomfort to cover any natural evidence that we are either. From puberty we are preoccupied with sex; but our courts, our counselors, and our psychiatrists are dealing constantly with cases of sexual failure or charges of frigidity or impotence. A small failure in business can quite normally make a man sexually impotent.

We fancy ourselves as hardheaded realists, but we will buy anything we see advertised, particularly on television; and we buy it not with reference to the quality or the value of the product, but directly as a result of the number of times we have heard it mentioned. The most arrant nonsense about a product is never questioned. We are afraid to be awake, afraid to be alone, afraid to be a moment without the noise and confusion we call entertainment. We boast of our dislike of highbrow art and music, and we have more and better-attended symphonies, art galleries, and theaters than any country in the world. We detest abstract art and produce more of it than all the rest of the world put together.

Follow-Up: Answer the following questions after you have read "Paradox and Dream." Discuss your answers with your classmates.

Comprehension:

Check those statements that accurately reflect information in the selection.

1. _____ Americans take their virtues to extremes.
2. _____ Americans have a positive self-image.
3. _____ Americans are realistic about themselves.
4. _____ Americans generally believe their government should be replaced.
5. _____ The most important part of an American's life is his/her family.
6. _____ The author of this piece has a positive view of Americans.

Fact/Opinion:

Check those statements that are facts. Do not mark opinions.

1. _____ The result is that we seem to be in a state of turmoil all the time, both physically and mentally.
2. _____ Fortunes are spent getting cats out of trees.
3. _____ There isn't a man among us in ten thousand who knows how to butcher a cow or a pig and cut it up for eating.

4. _____ We have more and better-attended symphonies, art galleries, and theaters than any country in the world.
5. _____ The most arrant nonsense about a product is never questioned.

Expectations:

Check only those assumptions that could be drawn from this reading, by someone who reads it before coming to America. Such a person could expect:

1. _____ To find few alcoholics in America.
2. _____ To find a lot of vegetarians in America.
3. _____ To meet a lot of people who want to give advice about the right way to do something.
4. _____ To find lazy workers in most companies.
5. _____ To hear Americans praise the government a lot.
6. _____ To be encouraged by Americans to retain his/her own way of life.
7. _____ To be disturbed by American parent-child relationships.
8. _____ To hear Americans talk about buying more and better things for themselves.
9. _____ To be treated in a cold, rude way.
10. _____ To see Americans giving money to beggars.
11. _____ To see many beautiful gardens.
12. _____ To hear of many gun-related tragedies.
13. _____ To find sexual relations with Americans dissatisfying.
14. _____ To find Americans to be cautious consumers.

How to Write a Summary

After each of the readings in this book, there is at least one exercise that asks you to "summarize the reading in 75 to 100 words." A summary is a brief restatement *in your own words* of the main point and major divisions of the article. It is not all that difficult to write a summary if you keep the following points in mind:

1. The first sentence of the summary is the most important because it contains the main idea of the reading. The first sentence should contain all of the following: the name of the author and the title of the article, a verb that shows what the author *did* in the article, and a short restatement of the main idea. To decide the latter two parts, it might help to ask this question: why did the author write the article? The following is the first sentence of a summary about the article "Paradox and Dreams":

> *In the essay* Paradox and Dreams, *John Steinbeck shows, by means of many different examples, the conflicting sides of the American character.*

2.   After the initial sentence, the summary should mention the main parts of the reading without referring to any specific examples. It would probably be best to use the present tenses as much as possible. It often helps to pretend that you and a friend are having a conversation about your school work. Imagine that your friend says to you, "What have you been reading lately?" After you tell your friend the name of the work that you have been reading, your friend will probably ask you something like, "So what is it about?" Imagine your response to your friend in a situation where you only have *one minute* to tell him the main points. Those are the points that you should probably include in your summary. Remember, however, that your friend did not ask you, "So how do you like it?" Therefore, you will not tell your friend what you think of it. Personal opinion is never included in a summary. Also, since this is a conversation with a friend, you will probably be speaking from memory, rather than looking at the text. In that way, you will be using your own words rather than the author's words to state these main points.

The following are some general topics that Steinbeck covers in "Paradox and Dreams": the contrasts between what we think of ourselves and what we actually do, the differences between some of our national character traits and our behavior, and the American image versus the reality. You might have other main points that come to mind after you have reread the article. Reread the article and, with a classmate, practice asking yourselves the two important questions mentioned above. Then, write a short summary of the article, and compare your summary with the summaries of your classmates.

1

THE MELTING POT AND THE SALAD BOWL

Eugene Gordon

A. Who do you think is driving this buggy?

B. Why do you think the driver is using a buggy instead of a car?

C. How do you think the driver of the car feels?

D. Is there any group of people in your country that uses buggies?

INTRODUCTION

Vocabulary in Context

Directions: Read the following passage without using your dictionary. As you read the passage, try to guess the meaning of the following words, all of which have been underlined in the passage. Write your guesses in the appropriate column and when you have finished reading, look up the words in an English-English dictionary to check your guesses. Then reread the passage, using your dictionary, and do the exercises at the end of the passage.

Words	My Guess	Dictionary Definition
proponents		
analogy		
distinguish		
ingredient		

Americans are a diverse group of people—a combination of Native Americans, sometimes called American Indians, and the descendants of immigrants from many lands. Most of the immigrants before World War II were from Europe; since that time, however, the immigrants have come mostly from Latin America and Asia. Two theories exist about the role of these immigrants in American society.

One theory, called the Melting Pot Theory, holds that new immigrants should blend—in a sense, melt—into the culture and become like the other people in the society. Proponents of this theory draw an analogy, or a comparison, to a melting pot. If gold and silver coins are thrown into a melting pot, it is impossible to distinguish what was originally gold and what was originally silver. So should it be with immigrants. Proponents of the melting pot believe that immigrants should "become American" so that it will be impossible to distinguish who was originally African, or European, or Asian.

The other theory about immigrants is the Salad Bowl Theory. Proponents of the Salad Bowl Theory claim that new immigrants should be encouraged to maintain their uniqueness while at the same time contributing to the total "flavor" of American life. They point out that in a salad, a tomato plays two roles: that of a tomato and that of a salad <u>ingredient.</u> Immigrants, the Salad Bowl theorists say, should retain their cultural individuality while contributing to American society.

So whose theory is best? What works best? What do people prefer? Maybe you'll have a few ideas about answers to these questions after you finish this chapter.

Reading for Full Comprehension

1. What is another word used in this passage that means the same as "uniqueness?"

2. The Melting Pot Theory compares immigrants to _____.

3. The Salad Bowl Theory compares immigrants to _____.

4. Proponents of the Salad Bowl Theory would probably compare American society to a _____.

READING #1

Prereading

Directions: These are some of the words that you will need to understand before reading the passage.

The Reformation: a division in Christianity that occurred in the sixteenth century in Europe. Sometimes called the Protestant Reformation.

William Penn: an English religious reformer who established the colony (which later became the state) of Pennsylvania. He started the colony with the idea that it would be a refuge for victims of religious persecution in Europe.

Vocabulary in Context

Directions: Read the following passage without using your dictionary. As you read the passage, try to guess the meaning of the following words, all of which have been underlined in the passage. Write your guesses in the appropriate column and after you have finished reading, look up the words in an English-English dictionary to check your guesses. Then reread the passage, using your dictionary, and do the exercises at the end of the passage.

Words	My Guess	Dictionary Definition
eschews		
trappings		
driving		
emigrate		
bewildering		
shunned		
congregations		

Words	My Guess	Dictionary Definition
cluster		
predominate		
intrusion		
focus		

THE PLAIN PEOPLE OF PENNSYLVANIA

by Doug Lee

Adapted from: National Geographic, April 1984, pp. 492–519.

1   The home of the Amish is Lancaster County, Pennsylvania, where they and their
2 ancestors have farmed for more than two hundred years. Their way of life is the plain way,
3 a life that eschews many of the trappings of the modern world. The roots of their religion
4 reach back to sixteenth-century Switzerland, where the Anabaptists, preachers of adult
5 baptism, were persecuted for nonconformism, driving many to emigrate. The strength of
6 their beliefs is seen today in a culture that thrives on the borders of urban America but
7 remains true to teachings of Reformation Europe.
8   Neighbors in faith and geography, Old Order Mennonites and other groups also
9 practice plain ways. Differences in work, home life, and worship are bewildering to an
10 outsider. Some churches allow members cars, electricity, and their own telephones—all
11 three forbidden to Old Order Amish and the most conservative Mennonites. But all share
12 the same strong foundations: a common dialect of German, often mistakenly called
13 "Pennsylvania Dutch"; unshakeable devotion to God: and firm devotion to "our people."
14   Jacob Amman led his followers—the Amish—out of the Mennonite Church in 1693,
15 principally because it no longer shunned nonconforming members from daily life as

16 Simons had taught. Shunning is still used by modern Amish, who exclude members for
17 nonconformism, such as marrying people from outside the faith. Nonetheless, both
18 groups remain close in spiritual beliefs, their lives centered on their church community. In
19 both, those <u>congregations</u> that have most resisted change in lifestyle and worship are today
20 called the Old Order.
21   Amish settlements in Lancaster County <u>cluster</u> thickest in the south, while Old Order
22 Mennonites <u>predominate</u> in the north. For many years now, a booming tourist trade is an
23 unwanted <u>intrusion</u> that has sprung up in the country. The Plain People are the unwilling
24 <u>focus</u> of tourist attention. The curiosity of outsiders, whom the Amish call the "English," is
25 unwelcome to a people for whom privacy is part of their religion.

Reading for Full Comprehension

1. T/F   The Amish and the Mennonites were originally both Anabaptists.

2. T/F   It is implied that, at one time, adult baptism was considered unusual.

3. T/F   The most liberal groups of Amish and Mennonites are called "Old Order."

4. T/F   Amish and Mennonites "shun" members who don't conform.

5. T/F   There are only two groups of Plain People in Lancaster County: Amish and Mennonites.

6. T/F   The Plain People were originally not wanted in Pennsylvania.

7. T/F   The Amish and the Mennonites speak Dutch.

8. T/F   A member of the Old Order Amish would probably not have a driver's license.

9. T/F   Most of the tourists in Lancaster County are British.

10.   Summarize this reading selection in 75 to 100 words.

THE MOVIE: WITNESS

Photofest

A. Who do you think these people are?

B. Are there people in your country who dress like this?

About the Movie

Directions: Following the instructions at the end of the passage, divide this passage into phrases and practice reading it aloud. Then, discuss it with a classmate.

The movie starts at the funeral of an Amish farmer, Jacob Lapp. After the funeral, his widow, Rachel Lapp, and son, Samuel Lapp, go to Baltimore to visit her sister. They take the train to Philadelphia, but their connecting train is delayed. While they are waiting in the train station, Samuel witnesses a murder in the men's bathroom. A policeman is knifed by two men, one white and one black. Captain John Book of the Philadelphia Police Department and his partner, Sergeant Carter, are called to investigate the crime. Imagine Book's surprise when Samuel Lapp identifies a policeman, Lieutenant McFee of the narcotics division, as the black man he saw murder the policeman in the bathroom.

Phrasing:

Dividing your reading into phrases helps you to improve your oral reading and your reading speed. There are three types of phrases in English: noun phrases, verb phrases, and prepositional phrases. A noun phrase consists of a noun and all its adjectives (and adjective clauses); a verb phrase consists of a verb and its complement or object; and a prepositional phrase consists of a preposition and its object. The first sentence can be divided in many ways.

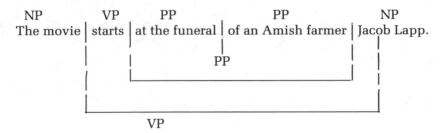

The larger your phrases, the more natural your reading will sound. Read each phrase straight through without pausing. Take breaths only between phrases.

Cultural Points About the Movie

In the United States, doctors, or other medical personnel, are required by law to report to the police if they treat a person with a gunshot wound.

Movie Vocabulary

Directions: These are some words that you will need to understand before seeing the movie. Look them up in your dictionary, or ask an American friend for the definitions. Write the letter of the correct definition in front of each word.

1. _____ **barn-raising** (gerund):
2. _____ **Bishop** (noun):
3. _____ **Elders** (noun):
4. _____ **hooks and eyes** (noun):
5. _____ **quaint** (adj.):
6. _____ **runt** (noun):
7. _____ **speed** (noun):
8. _____ **whacking** (gerund/participle):

a. the head of a group of churches

b. a type of metal, clothing fastener used in place of buttons.

c. a type of narcotic used as a stimulant

d. the oldest, most important men in a single church

e. an Amish activity in which a barn is built by all members of the community.

f. a small person or animal

g. hitting

h. interesting in an old-fashioned way.

As You Watch the Movie

Directions: Read the following questions; keep them in mind while you watch the movie. After the movie, discuss your answers to these questions with a small group of your classmates.

This is a movie about two cultures: the culture of the Amish and the culture of urban America. As you watch the movie, keep in mind the ways in which the director of the movie shows the differences between the two cultures. What points of contrast does he emphasize? How does he show the contrast? How do the people in the movie change as their cultures come into contact with one another? Which culture does the director seem to prefer?

Postmovie Discussion Questions

1. What is the division of labor in Amish society? What types of work do men do? What do women do? How is labor divided at an Amish social event, such as a funeral or a barn-raising?

2. What are some of the scenes in which the director contrasts the Amish way of life and the non-Amish way of life? What point does the director make in these scenes? How does he make the point?

3. What are the opinions of John, Rachel, Eli, and Samuel about the gun?

4. What is the Amish belief about violence and aggression? In which scenes is the point made?

5. What does John Book learn from the Amish? How does the director show this?

6. What do the Amish learn from John Book?

MOVIE REVIEW #1

Vocabulary in Context

Directions: Read the following passage without using your dictionary. As you read the passage, try to guess the meaning of the following words, all of which have been underlined in the passage. Write your guesses in the appropriate column and after you have finished reading, look up the words in an English-English dictionary to check your guesses. Then reread the passage, using your dictionary, and do the exercises at the end of the passage.

Words	My Guess	Dictionary Definition
blackclad		
bide time		

Words	My Guess	Dictionary Definition
brutal		
cops		
dope ring		
do in		
unworldly		
detained		
sidekick		
doused		
idyllic		
fornicating		
chaste		

Words	My Guess	Dictionary Definition
sleaziness		
baubles		
superior		
shootout		
malefactors		
leech		
remedies		
ringing up		
utters		
contemplate		
bumped off		

Words	My Guess	Dictionary Definition
dawn		
awkwardly		
glances		
ablutions		
bosom		
affair		
showdown		
sauntering		

FANCY MEETING PLAIN AGAIN

by John Simon

© *National Review, Inc.*, April 5, 1985, pp. 56–58. Reprinted by permission.

1   Peter Weir is far from being the most talented, but is surely the most successful,
2 current Australian filmmaker. The combination is unsurprising. With "Witness," Weir
3 ("Gallipoli," "The Year of Living Dangerously") has made his first American movie, and it
4 is no better, no less phony, than his Australian films. It is visually arresting, it has its
5 moments of melodramatic excitement, and it is about as artistic as "Waltzing Matilda"
6 played by a symphony orchestra.
7   "Witness" begins with an Amish funeral near Lancaster, Pennsylvania: Blackclad
8 Amish are walking through wheat. Newly widowed Rachel Lapp is off with Samuel, her
9 eight-year-old, to visit relatives in Baltimore. Having missed a connection in Philadelphia,
10 the two must bide their time in the railway waiting room. In the deserted men's room,
11 Samuel witnesses a brutal murder (all murders are brutal, but Weir's more so) in which two
12 cops who are part of a multimillion dollar dope ring do in a third. That small, unworldly
13 Samuel should be able to trick such experienced searchers into not discovering him
14 situates "Witness" in the realm of make-believe.
15   Rachel and Samuel are detained by the tough but honest police captain, John Book
16 (white), who, with his tough but honest sidekick (black), conducts the investigation.
17 Immediately, we are doused with contrasts: violent Philadelphia v. idyllic Lancaster, foul-
18 spoken Book v. clean-mouthed Rachel, Book's fornicating divorcee sister (with whom
19 John shelters the Lapps) v. the chaste Rachel—in short, urban sleaziness and dirt v.
20 country purity and piety. That these Amish live in 1985 as if it were 1800 (no telephones,
21 TV, radio, cars, even buttons, those devil's baubles fostering human pride) strikes the
22 filmmakers as wonderful. There is something distastefully disingenuous about the defer-
23 ence with which these filmmakers extol the exotic unworldliness of the Amish rustics.
24   Samuel identifies one of the murderous cops, and Book in turn discovers that his own
25 superior is running the dope ring. Severely wounded in a shootout with one of the
26 malefactors, Book yet manages to drive Rachel and Samuel back to the Lapp farm and
27 there passes out. After some perfunctory compunctions, a good Amish leech cures Book
28 with natural remedies and Rachel's devoted care. Soon John becomes like one of the true
29 Amish, even wearing the dead Lapp's clothes, which have to be way too short for him so
30 that he may look "plain" (the Amish term for humble and devout) in the eyes of God, and a
31 sight gag in the eyes of the audience. Rachel and John start falling in love despite Grandpa
32 Lapp's warning that she will end up being "shunned" (ostracized), after he catches them
33 dancing in the nocturnal barn by the lights and radio of John's car.
34   Though Book's recovery is now complete, he does nothing about the dope ring
35 beyond ringing up his partner from the area's general store. (The film's only good line is

36 Rachel's telling John that the nearest phone is miles away on the farm of some—she utters
37 the word with mild contempt—Mennonites.) Book and his partner contemplate calling
38 the FBI or the press but do nothing, whereupon the partner is bumped off. Book makes a
39 threatening phone call to his murderous boss, but still does nothing else. The film
40 proceeds to explore the joys of plain living, such as getting up before dawn to milk the
41 cows, which Book does awkwardly; carpentering, which he does better; and exchanging
42 loving glances with Rachel, at which he is best, especially at a barn-raising at which he
43 carpenters and she waits on the communal tables.
44   But more than barns, hopes are being raised here as Rachel, one stormy night, is
45 caught by Book during her evening ablutions, and with unaffected innocence, reveals her
46 bosom to him. But Book leaves her as untouched as the dope ring, explaining that, were he
47 to yield, either she would have to leave or he would have to stay. This would not do—at
48 least not that night. But a couple of nights later the affair is consummated, with neither of
49 the aforementioned consequences. Instead, the bad guys come to get Book, and there is a
50 showdown, marginally more thrilling than the barn raising. Now Book does have to leave,
51 but coming in the opposite direction is the fine young Amish fellow (played by the Russian
52 dancer Alexander Godunov) who all along was waiting to wed Rachel. A bittersweet
53 ending, markedly and marketably more sweet than bitter.
54   Even the Amish speech is inconsistent here, let alone the thinking. When Rachel and
55 John are dancing and romancing, emancipation seems to be the proper thing. But when
56 herbal healing works wonders, when Book carves a new birdhouse, and when at the end
57 Godunov comes sauntering toward Rachel, the primitive proves sublime. Rachel and John
58 have had their sweet fling and can share a rapturous memory, then let each other proceed
59 along his nicely preordained path.
60   Harrison Ford does a decent, solid job of Book, but Kelley McGillis is a real drama-
61 school actress (as she was also in the dreadful "Reuben, Reuben)." Though she is very
62 pretty from some angles, the moment her cast-iron jaw takes over the screen, she might as
63 well be some country weather vane. Godunov knows how to look intensely casual, and little
64 Lukas is good as golden wheat as Samuel. If film were, as is sometimes asserted, a purely
65 visual medium, the visuals might be enough. But it isn't and they aren't.

Reading for Full Comprehension

1. To what do the words "the combination" (line 2) refer to?

2. To what do the words "the aforementioned consequences" (line 49) refer to?

3. To what do the words "it isn't" and "they aren't" (line 65) refer to?

4. What does the author think about Weir's Australian films (lines 4, 5, 6)? What does he think about Witness?"

5. What does the author think about Weir's use of violence in movies (line 11)?

6. How realistic does the author think Witness is (lines 12, 13, 14)?

7. What is the author's opinion about the filmmaker's opinion of the Amish (lines 22, 23)?

8. In lines 34, 38, 46, the author repeats the point that on several occasions John Book took no action. What opinion is the author indirectly trying to express by pointing out these examples?

9. How exciting does the author think the movie is (line 50)?

10. What does the author think about the movie's realism (lines 53, 54)? What examples does he use to make his point?

11. What is the author's opinion of the looks and performance of the actress Kelley McGillis (lines 60, 61, 62, 63)?

12. In fifty words or less, summarize the basic opinions of the author about this movie.

13. Summarize this reading selection in 75 to 100 words.

MOVIE REVIEW #2

Prereading

Directions: These are some words you will need to understand before reading the passage.

time-warp (compound noun): a place where things do not change. A place where time seems to "stand still."

trick logic (compound noun): a type of thinking that is not ordinary or usual.

Vocabulary in Context

Directions: Read the following passage without using your dictionary. As you read the passage, try to guess the meaning of the following words, all of which have been underlined in the passage. Write your guesses in the appropriate column and after you have finished reading, look up the words in an English-English dictionary to check your guesses. Then reread the passage, using your dictionary, and do the exercises at the end of the passage.

Words	My Guess	Dictionary Definition
thrills		
scuzzy		
crooked		
pastoral		
pious		
corrupt		
consternation		
anxiety		

Words	My Guess	Dictionary Definition
track down		
hideout		
incongruous		
communal		
swarms		
hardened		
vicious		
lock eyes with		

A CITY COP IN AMISH COUNTRY

by Jack Kroll

From: *Newsweek*, February 11, 1985. © 1985, *Newsweek, Inc.* All rights reserved.
Reprinted by permission.

1   What you want from a thriller, besides <u>thrills,</u> is a little originality, a MacGuffin, as
2 Hitchcock called it, to beguile you with its trick logic. You get that—and more—in
3 "Witness." The original screenplay by Earl. W. Wallace and William Kelley brings together
4 the <u>scuzzy,</u> violent, urban world of narcotics, murder, and <u>crooked</u> cops and the <u>pastoral,</u>
5 time-warp world of the Amish, those <u>pious,</u> blackclad Pennsylvania farmers who live today
6 much as they did in the seventeenth century. While on a trip with his widowed mother
7 Rachel (Kelley McGillis), Samuel Lapp, a little Amish boy (Lukas Haas), witnesses a brutal
8 murder in the men's room of a Philadelphia railway station. John Book (Harrison Ford),
9 the detective assigned to the case, discovers that the killers are <u>corrupt</u> cops. When they
10 put a bullet into him, Book escapes to Amish country. Peace. Beauty. John loves Rachel.
11 Vice versa. <u>Consternation</u> among the Amish. <u>Anxiety</u> among the crooked cops, who finally
12 <u>track</u> John <u>down</u> in his idyllic <u>hideout.</u> Climactic, cross-cultural crunch.
13   Not every director could make this unlikely situation work. But Australia's Peter
14 Weir, making his first American-based film, does an admirable job. In his Australian
15 movies, like "Picnic at Hanging Rock" and "The Last Wave" he's dealt with mystery,
16 murder, and the clash of <u>incongruous</u> cultures. The aborigines in "The Last Wave" are
17 like the Amish in "Witness"—both groups, isolated in the modern world, have retained an
18 almost mystic spiritual integrity. But, Weir has lost much of his portentousness while
19 losing none of his extraordinary artistry. "Witness" is a feast of ravishing images and
20 suspenseful rhythms: at a <u>communal</u> barn-raising, the half-built barn <u>swarms</u> with men,
21 like bees making honey; at the police station, when Samuel identifies a photograph of the
22 killers for John Book, Weir goes into sudden slow motion, creating an electric intimacy
23 between the innocent boy and the <u>hardened</u> cop.
24   **Portrait:** As he showed in "The Year of Living Dangerously," in which he cast actress
25 Linda Hunt as the male half-caste Billy Kwan, Weir has a wonderful eye for the
26 unexpected. Here Alexander Godunov, the Russian ballet dancer who defected to the
27 United States, is immensely engaging as a young Amish farmer who has his eye on Rachel.
28 Weir is superb with actors: Lukas Haas is angelic but real as Samuel; Josef Sommer seems
29 to sweat evil as Book's crooked chief; you can't believe that Danny Glover, the saintly
30 sharecropper of "Places in the Heart," is the <u>vicious</u> murderer in this movie; Harrison
31 Ford is tough, sweet, romantic, brooding, masculine—more like the easy-flowing old
32 movie stars than almost anybody in his generation. And Kelley McGillis as Rachel is the
33 most incandescent young actress to come along in a while. In her severe Amish dress she
34 has the solidity and sensuality of a Frans Hals portrait. Turning from her bath to <u>lock eyes</u>

35 with Ford, she makes one of the screen's most beautiful and moving shots of a woman—
36 the embodiment of T. S. Eliot's line "The awful daring of a moment's surrender."

Reading for Full Comprehension

1. What does the word "that" (line 2) refer to?

2. What do the words "this unlikely situation" (line 13) refer to?

3. The author of this passage follows a pattern of making a general, opinion statement and supporting it with several examples to support his opinion.

    A. In lines 3 to 6, beginning with the words "The original screen-play . . . ," he gives one set of examples. What sentence is the general, opinion statement for these examples? Underline that sentence.

    B. In lines 20 to 22, beginning with the words "at a communal barn-raising . . . ," he gives another set of examples. What sentence is the general opinion statement for these examples? Underline that sentence. What punctuation mark is used between the general statement and the examples?

    C. In lines 24 to 26, beginning with the words "As he showed . . . ," he gives another set of examples. What part of a sentence is the general opinion statement for these examples? Underline that sentence.

    D. In lines 28 to 33, beginning with the words "Lukas Haas is . . . ," he gives another set of examples. What sentence is the general opinion statement for these examples? Underline that sentence. What punctuation mark is used between the general statement and the examples?

4. Now look at the four opinion statements you found in number 3 A–D. Using your own words, summarize the opinion of the author about the movie in 75 to 100 words.

WRITING ASSIGNMENTS

1. Write a letter to a friend in your country, describing the Plain People of Pennsylvania. In separate paragraphs, explain and describe their background, their way of life, their social events, their beliefs, and anything else about them that your friend might find interesting.

2. Watch the murder scene in the bathroom. Pretend that you are Samuel. Write a brief, one paragraph report in which you describe what you experienced in the bathroom.

3. Return to the concept of the Melting Pot and the Salad Bowl. Consider that these two theories can be applied to any society's treatment of immigrants. Think about how the Amish live in the framework of United States society. Think about how the Amish treat people who enter their culture. Write a paragraph explaining the Salad Bowl theory and illustrate it with examples from what you have learned about the Amish. Then, write another paragraph explaining the Melting Pot theory and illustrate it with other examples from what you have learned about the Amish.

4. Consider the fact that the movie *Witness* was very popular in the United States. Also consider the fact that the Amish value their privacy. Pretend that you are a member of the Amish. How would you feel about this movie? Pretend that you are a non-Amish member of Lancaster County Chamber of Commerce. How would you feel about this movie? Write two essays. In the first essay, pretend you are Amish. You are writing a letter to the editor of the Lancaster County newspaper, expressing your opinion about the movie. Start with a clear thesis sentence in which you express your opinion about the movie. Then, pick two or three reasons to support your opinion, and develop each reason in a paragraph. Then, pretend that you are the non-Amish member of the Lancaster County Chamber of Commerce. Write a letter to the editor, expressing your opinion about the movie. Start with a clear thesis sentence in which you express your opinion about the movie. Then pick two or three reasons to support your opinion and develop each reason in a paragraph.

5. Write a paragraph in which you explain some fundamental belief or practice of the Amish. Then, write another paragraph in which you explain how the non-Amish could benefit from adopting it.

6. Write a paragraph on the role and position of women in Amish society. Then, write another paragraph in which you compare/contrast it with the role and position of women in non-Amish, American society.

7. Almost every country has ethnic minorities. Some of these minorities "melt in" to the society and some do not. Think about your own country's ethnic minorities. Is there one in particular that does not "melt in" but remains separate from the general culture? If there is, write an essay about that minority. In the first paragraph, identify the minority. Why is it a minority? Is it a racial, religious, or economic minority? Does it remain apart from the general culture by choice, or is it forced to remain apart? In the second paragraph, identify one distinguishing feature of the minority. Maybe it is a custom, a tradition, a way of dress, or a language. Describe the distinguishing feature. In the third paragraph, begin with an opinion sentence in which you state the attitudes of the people in your country toward the minority. Explain the attitude and give examples.

8. State your opinion about the Amish attitude toward violence, guns, and war. Then, explain in separate paragraphs two or three reasons why you have this opinion.

9. Consider the role of immigrants in your country. How do most immigrants in your country fit into society? Is your country more of a Melting Pot or a Salad Bowl? State your opinion, and in separate paragraphs, give at least two different examples of immigrant groups in your country and how they have adapted to life in your country.

10. Consider the immigrants who live in your country. How has your country changed because of its immigrants? How has your country become a better or a worse place to live because of its immigrants? Write a thesis sentence in which you state the impact that immigrants have had on your country. Then, in two or three paragraphs show the different impacts that immigrants have had on your country.

11. Consider the issue of bilingualism versus monolingualism. Some say that as a country the United States should strive to be a bilingual nation. Others argue that we should concentrate on teaching English and let people who want to be bilingual speak their own languages at home. What do you think? Which is a more realistic goal for the United States? Explain your opinion in a paragraph with a clearly worded thesis sentence. Then, develop two or three paragraphs in which you explain your reasons for your opinion.

2

RETHINKING DISABILITIES

Laima Druskis

A. What are these people doing?

B. How do you think they feel?

INTRODUCTION

Prereading

*Directions: These are some words that you will need to understand before reading
the passage.*

The civil rights movement (compound noun): A popular movement in the1950s
and the 1960s, during which time blacks, and members of other minorities, demanded their civil rights. Civil rights are the basic rights that any
citizen of the United States is entitled to.

Vocabulary in Context

*Directions: Read the following passage without using your dictionary. As you read
the passage, try to guess the meaning of the following words, all of which
are underlined in the passage. Write your guesses in the appropriate
column and look up the words in an English-English dictionary to check
your guesses. Then reread the passage, using your dictionary, and do the
exercises at the end of the passage.*

Words	My Guess	Dictionary Definition
come to mind		
constitute		
legislative		
ramps		

Words	My Guess	Dictionary Definition
orthopedically		
Braille		
close captioned		

Find three words in the passage that are used to refer to people with hearing problems.

1   Racial, ethnic, or religious minorities, such as the Amish, <u>come</u> <u>to</u> <u>mind</u> first when
2 most people think of minorities. However, the handicapped also <u>constitute</u> a minority.
3 There are deaf or hard-of-hearing, blind or visually handicapped, mute or speech-
4 impaired, mentally retarded, emotionally disturbed, and orthopedically or other health-
5 impaired people. Since the civil rights movement of the 1960s, the handicapped have
6 become more active in demanding their civil rights. Consequently, some of the laws have
7 changed.
8   Thanks to these <u>legislative</u> changes, we can now observe many physical changes in
9 public places. There are now special parking places, access <u>ramps</u> to buildings, doors with
10 buttons to open them automatically, and restrooms equipped with special toilet seats for
11 the <u>orthopedically</u> handicapped. Elevator buttons have special marks in <u>Braille</u> for the
12 visually impaired. Some television programs are <u>close</u> <u>captioned,</u> and charges on our
13 phone bill help to pay for teletype equipment that translate the phone messages for the
14 hearing impaired.
15   However, changes need to occur that are greater than just a few physical structures or
16 laws. Attitudes of the majority in this country must change if the handicapped are to be
17 fully accepted members of society. The most noticeable change in attitudes toward the
18 handicapped has occurred in the field of education—although, as you will see, more
19 changes are still needed.

Reading for Full Comprehension

1. T/F   Most people usually think of the handicapped when they think of minorities.

2. T/F   There is more than one type of hearing problem that can classify a person as handicapped.

3. T/F   The author would probably agree that civil rights laws have changed most people's attitudes toward the handicapped.

4. T/F   A person has to have a physical problem to be considered handicapped.

READING #1

Vocabulary in Context

Directions: *Read the following passage without using your dictionary. As you read the passage, try to guess the meaning of the following words, all of which are underlined in the passage. Write your guesses in the appropriate column and then look up the words in an English-English dictionary to check your guesses. Then reread the passage, using your dictionary, and do the exercises at the end of the passage.*

Words	My Guess	Dictionary Definition
phenomenon		
custodial		
dawning		
settings		
playing a key role		
to tailor		

Words	My Guess	Dictionary Definition
segregated		
severity		

EDUCATION FOR THE HANDICAPPED

by John A. Glover and Roger H. Bruning

1   Public school programs for handicapped students are a relatively recent phenome-
2 non. By the late nineteenth century, states began to accept responsibility for the care and
3 better treatment of handicapped individuals.
4   By the late nineteenth century, a number of private, city, or state-run institutions or
5 "homes" had been established to provide residential care for handicapped individuals. In
6 most instances, this care was more custodial than educational. Institutionalization often
7 meant hope had been lost and custodial care was "all that could be done" for a hand-
8 icapped person. A positive feature of this period, nonetheless, was a dawning recognition
9 of the special needs of handicapped persons.
10   Residential care is still a major part of services to the handicapped, particularly those
11 with severe disabilities. This care has been regulated more and more carefully, programs
12 have been initiated to meet the individual needs of the residents, and there is now the
13 potential of leaving institutions for settings that integrate the handicapped into the
14 community. Although there are some exceptions, residential facilities are no longer
15 viewed as places where residents are permanently housed, but rather they are seen as
16 places where people can develop skills that allow them to function outside the institutions.
17   At the turn of the twentieth century, public schools began to establish special classes
18 for handicapped students, particularly mildly retarded and physically handicapped
19 children. By the 1960s there were tens of thousands of special classes in the United States.
20 Placement in these classes was based on the identification and labeling of children, with
21 intelligence testing playing a key role in this process. Schools attempted to tailor classes to

22 the needs of handicapped students by having separate classes for groups such as "trainable
23 mentally retarded," "educable mentally retarded," and "learning disabled" students.
24   As services to the handicapped increased, however, so did the expectations for
25 improvement. The solutions of the 1950s and 1960s, especially <u>segregated</u> classrooms,
26 were increasingly questioned. Educators began to search for new ways to educate
27 handicapped students.
28   Rather than automatically teaching students in special classes, educators reasoned,
29 why not try to find a **least restrictive environment** for each handicapped student? The
30 least restrictive environment is defined as the program or setting that provides the greatest
31 opportunity for the individual development of a handicapped student—emotionally,
32 socially, or intellectually. What is least restrictive of his or her handicap for a particular
33 student depends on the nature and <u>severity</u> of his or her handicap and on what is available
34 in a school system.

Reading for Full Comprehension

1. T/F Residential care in the nineteenth century primarily provided educa-
         tion and training for the handicapped.

2. T/F The author would disagree that no real progress was made for the
         handicapped in the nineteenth century.

3. T/F Residential care is no longer provided to the handicapped.

4. T/F Special education classes started in the 1950s and 1960s.

5. T/F Children placed in special education classes were often severely
         retarded.

6. T/F Persons leaving institutions must go directly into society.

7. T/F Special education classes probably did not result in as much improve-
         ment as expected.

8. T/F The "least restrictive environment" depends on the nature and degree
         of handicap of each individual student and on the resources of the
         school.

9. T/F Summarize this reading selection in 75 to 100 words.

READING #2

Vocabulary in Context

Directions: *Read the following passage without using your dictionary. As you read the passage, try to guess the meaning of the following words, all of which are underlined in the passage. Write your guesses in the appropriate column and then look up the words in an English-English dictionary to check your guesses. After that, reread the passage, using your dictionary, and do the exercises at the end of the passage.*

Words	My Guess	Dictionary Definition
mainstreaming		
classified		
profoundly		
consultants		
injustices		
spell out		

Words	My Guess	Dictionary Definition

extent

consultation

THE IMPACT OF PUBLIC LAW 94-142

---

by Thomas L. Good and Jere E. Brophy

From: Educational Psychology: A Realistic Approach. Copyright © 1990 by Longman Publishing Group. Reprinted by permission of Longman Publishing Group.

1   Public Law 94-142, the Education for All Handicapped Children Act, was signed by
2 the president in 1975 but did not become effective until Fall 1977. The law called for a
3 number of sweeping changes, although its implementation was left primarily to individual
4 states, and there has been considerable variation among states.
5   In short, this law commits the nation to a policy of mainstreaming handicapped by
6 placing them in the least restrictive environment in which they will be able to function and
7 still have their special needs met. There is increasing resistance to removing students from
8 regular classrooms unless there is a clear need for a special program.
9   The least restrictive environment implies that special students are not to be classified
10 by handicap and given permanent special placement on the basis of their classification, but
11 instead are to be moved to special stations only if they require it and only for as long as
12 necessary. Profoundly deaf children, for example, usually will require full-time special
13 schools or special classes, but children with less severe hearing problems and children with
14 a variety of vision problems can spend part or even all of their time in regular classrooms,
15 although probably with some assistance from consultants or itinerant specialists. When
16 P.L. 94-142 was passed, some people thought that it called for all handicapped students to
17 be placed in regular classrooms, regardless of their type and severity of handicap. This
18 mistake was understandable because the bill's language emphasized correcting past
19 injustices as well as the right of all handicapped children to an appropriate education. The
20 key term in here is "appropriate," which is defined in terms of the least restrictive
21 environment. Thus, the law does not eliminate special education settings or require that
22 all students be placed in regular classrooms.
23   Public Law 94-142 does not fully spell out its implementation. This will be determined
24 gradually by court decisions, state laws, and local practices (Hansen, 1976).[1] The law does

[1] Hansen, K. (December 1976) *Implications of P.L. 94–142 for Higher Education.* A paper presented at the Regional Mainstreaming Conference, Kansas City, MO.

25 place six major requirements on state programs as a condition for obtaining federal
26 support:

27 1. Handicapped students must be educated to the maximum <u>extent</u> appropiate,
28   in the least restrictive environment.

29 2. Nondiscriminatory, culture-free testing in the native language of the students
30   is necessary prior to placement in special programs.

31 3. Prior <u>consultation</u> with parents must take place before special placement.

32 4. An individual education plan (IEP) must be prepared specifically for each
33   handicapped student.

34 5. Public school programs must serve nonpublic school students if they are
35   handicapped and require services that the federal government funds.

36 6. Staff development programs must be conducted in every school district.

Reading for Full Comprehension

1. Find five words in the passage that mean "special education."

2. Find two other words in the passage that mean "law."

3. What does "this mistake" in lines 17, 18 refer to?

4. T/F The way Wyoming implements P.L. 94-142 must be the same as the way Idaho implements it.

5. T/F The principle of the least restrictive environment is a function of the principle of mainstreaming.

6. T/F Under P.L. 94-142 placement in special education classes is permanent for all handicapped children.

7. T/F Schools that do not comply with P.L. 94-142 probably won't get money from the U.S. government.

8. T/F P.L. 94-142 dictates how programs for the handicapped should be implemented.

9. T/F According to P.L. 94-142 students must be tested in English.

10. T/F Parents play a role in the implementation of P.L. 94-142.

11. T/F Only students in public schools can benefit from P.L. 94-142.

12. T/F This text was probably written several years after P.L. 94-142 was written.

13. Summarize this reading selection in 75 to 100 words.

READING #3

Vocabulary in Context

Directions: Read the following passage without using your dictionary. As you read the passage, try to guess the meaning of the following words, all of which are underlined in the passage. Write your guesses in the appropriate column and then look up the words in an English-English dictionary to check your guesses. Afterwards, reread the passage, using your dictionary, and do the exercises at the end of the passage.

Words	My Guess	Dictionary Definition
partial		
perception		
perceive		
hearing aids		
deciphering		
span		
significant		

Words	My Guess	Dictionary Definition
gestural		
fluent		
meaningful		

HARD OF HEARING AND DEAF STUDENTS

by John A. Glover and Roger H. Bruning

Adapted from: "Hard of Hearing and Deaf Students" on pp. 609–611. From *Educational Psychology: Principles and Applications,* 2nd ed. Copyright © 1987 by John A. Glover and Roger H. Bruning. Reprinted by permission of Harper-Collins Publishers.

1 These two categories, although quite similar, are usually considered separately. Hard
2 of hearing students have <u>partial</u> hearing, while deaf students have no functional hearing
3 at all. Hearing impairment may range from mild to severe. Mild hearing impairment may
4 affect <u>perception</u> of only distant or faint sounds. Mildly impaired students may <u>perceive</u>
5 nearby sounds or normal conversation, although they may need <u>hearing aids</u>. In severe
6 hearing loss and deafness, even the loudest sounds are not heard.
7 About five children per thousand have hearing problems that require special atten-
8 tion in school, and of these a significant proportion may require special classes in speech
9 reading (which involves <u>deciphering</u> the lip, face, and throat movements of speakers) or
10 the use of sign language. The typical teacher might expect to have one or two hearing-
11 impaired or deaf students over a three- or four-year <u>span</u>.
12 Most students with more than mild hearing impairment require <u>significant</u> amounts
13 of time in special classrooms or schools in which skills in signing and speech reading are
14 learned. In signing (signed communication), the language is <u>gestural.</u> American Sign
15 Language, for example, is used by about a half-million deaf persons in the United States
16 alone (Benderly, 1980)[1], although many schools concentrate on signed English, a gestural

[1] Benderly, B. L. (1980). Dialogue of the deaf. *Psychology Today,* 66–77.

17 language that relates signs to English-language equivalents. Speech reading is often useful
18 if there is some functional hearing. To enable the more severely hearing-impaired
19 students to take part in regular classroom activities, a teacher-interpreter <u>fluent</u> in signed
20 communication is usually needed. Regular classroom teachers who have learned some
21 sign language have found that their ability to use signs has opened up a whole range of
22 communication with hearing-impaired students in their classes. Additionally, many
23 schools now teach some signing to their normal-hearing students to make possible more
24 <u>meaningful</u> relationships with deaf and hard-of-hearing students.

Reading for Full Comprehension

1. List some of the differences between hearing impairment and deafness.

Difference	Deaf	Hearing-Impaired

2. T/F   There are three gestural languages used by the deaf.

3. T/F   American Sign Language is different from signed English.

4. T/F   Speech reading is probably not as useful to the deaf as it is to the
         hearing-impaired.

5. T/F   Hearing students don't have any reason to learn sign language.

6. T/F   Partial hearing could be defined as some functional hearing.

7. T/F   This passage was probably written for deaf students.

8. Summarize this reading selection in 75 to 100 words.

READING #4

Prereading

***Directions: These are some words that you will need to understand before reading
the passage.***

Selma: (proper name): Selma is a town in Alabama. During the 1960s, a large
civil rights demonstration and march took place there.

Vocabulary in Context

Directions: *Read the following passage without using your dictionary. As you read the passage, try to guess the meaning of the following words, all of which are underlined in the passage. Write your guesses in the appropriate column and then look up the words in an English-English dictionary to check your guesses. Afterwards, reread the passage using your dictionary and do the exercises at the end of the passage.*

Words	My Guess	Dictionary Definition
tribute		
turning out		
passed over		
called it quits		
stead		
the push		
militancy		
contended		

Words	My Guess	Dictionary Definition
attributed to		
resentment		
paternalistic		
appropriated		
to press for		
cheered		
activists		
disabled		
to underscore		
transit		
accessible		

Words	My Guess	Dictionary Definition
poll		
rallying point		
inaccessible		
obstacle		
to pick up on		
parallels		

Keeping in mind that the Latin root "pater" means "father," define "paternalism" in your own words. Then, give an example of paternalism from the article. What is the adjective form of this word?

A CRY FROM THE DEAF IS HEARD IN WASHINGTON

From: "A Cry from the Deaf Is Heard in Washington," *U.S. News & World Report,* March 21, 1988: 9–10.

1   Gallaudet University in Washington, D.C. is often called "the Harvard of deaf
2 people"—a tribute to its academic excellence and long-time tradition of turning out role
3 models for people who are deaf. But last week, when the school's search for a new
4 president passed over two hearing-impaired candidates, student protesters defiantly shut
5 down the campus of red-brick buildings one mile from the U.S. Capitol. After four days of
6 demonstrations, the new president, Elisabeth Ann Zinser, called it quits, and the school's

7 trustees began looking for an administrator, most likely a deaf one, in her stead. Why the
8 push for a hearing-impaired president at a school that had never had one before in its 124-
9 year history?
10   The calls for a deaf president sprang from a growing militancy by people with
11 disabilities. At issue for protesters at Gallaudet was a feeling that the trustees had, in fact,
12 decided that a deaf person was not capable of running the school. Some angry students
13 contended that the chairman of the school's board of trustees, Jane Bassett Spilman, had
14 told them, "Deaf people are not ready to function in a hearing world." Spilman, with a
15 long record of work in the deaf community, vigorously denied making the statement,
16 which she attributed to a misunderstanding during a conversation through interpreters.
17 Nevertheless, the dispute showed students' simmering resentment of what they called the
18 "paternalistic" attitude of the school's trustees, only a minority of whom are themselves
19 deaf. "We need a role model for the deaf now," declared protest leader John Limnidis, "to
20 show that the deaf people can do it."
21   The pressure on Gallaudet—ranked No. 1 among Eastern liberal-arts colleges in *U.S.
22 News*'s 1987 college survey and the only liberal-arts college in the world for deaf people—
23 came not only from unhappy students but from deaf people around the country, most of
24 the faculty, and key legislators as well. Some 75 percent of the college's funds are
25 appropriated by Congress. The resignation of Zinser, an educator from the University of
26 North Carolina at Greensboro, did not end the protests. Students vowed to stay on campus
27 over the spring break to press for the removal of Spilman and for the appointment of
28 hearing-impaired persons to the board of trustees.
29   The fight of the students cheered activists for disabled groups across the United
30 States. "It is an example of what we all want—to end paternalism," said Mark Johnson of
31 American Disabled for Accessible Public Transportation (ADAPT). Members of ADAPT
32 were planning a protest of their own in Washington this week—pledging to get themselves
33 arrested for blocking traffic to underscore their demands that all public transit be made
34 accessible to wheelchair users.
35   More and more, disabled people have come to see their problems as one of civil rights.
36 A recent poll conducted for two disability groups found that 45 percent of disabled
37 Americans identify themselves as members of an oppressed minority. In fact, even the
38 politically conservative members of the National Council on the Handicapped have
39 drafted a wide-reaching bill to expand the rights of the disabled. That measure has
40 become a rallying point for disabled groups. They see prejudice against people with
41 disabilities—whether it is buildings made inaccessible or being turned away at a
42 restaurant—as a bigger obstacle than their physical disabilities. Gallaudet students were
43 quick to pick up on the parallels to the civil rights struggles of blacks in the 1960s. As
44 graduate student Kathy Karcher told students at a protest: "This is the Selma of the deaf."

Reading for Full Comprehension

1. Give another word that is used by the author to mean "deaf." Given what you have already learned in other readings, does he use this word correctly?

2. Give another word from the article that means the same thing as "a protest."

3. Give three other words from the article that mean the same as "the push for."

4. Give another word from the article used for "handicapped."

5. Give another word for "bill" used in the article.

6. According to the article, the deaf students are comparing themselves to

   _____.

7. T/F   Elisabeth Zinser is deaf.

8. T/F   At least three people were considered for the job of president at Gallaudet.

9. T/F   Gallaudet University is a part of Harvard.

10. T/F   Gallaudet University is the best college in the East according to *U.S. News*.

11. T/F   The author is somewhat surprised that the National Council of the Handicapped has drafted a bill to expand the rights of the handicapped.

12. T/F   Jane Bassett Spilman knows sign language.

13. T/F   The students had two demands that they demonstrated about.

14. T/F   Other handicapped people are also planning protests.

15. T/F   Most disabled Americans believe they are part of a minority group.

16. T/F   To people with disabilities, the biggest obstacle is their handicaps.

17. Summarize this reading selection in 75 to 100 words.

THE MOVIE: CHILDREN OF A LESSER GOD

Photofest

A. Who do you think these two people are?

B. What do you think the young woman is doing?

About the Movie

Directions: Divide the following reading into phrases. Then, practice reading it aloud. Following the directions at the end of the passage, determine where the primary stress should fall in word groups. Then, reread it and discuss it with a classmate.

James Leads, an idealistic teacher in a school for hearing-impaired students, thinks he can teach anyone to speak and read lips in order to function in the hearing world. The majority of the students, trying to overcome their handicap, enjoy his innovative techniques of teaching speech. At first, the school principal, Franklin, is quite unresponsive to him, but seeing James's positive influence on the students, he finally begins to accept him.

Sarah Norman, a beautiful, bright deaf-mute woman with a fiery temperament is a graduate of the school. She is still on campus doing menial work. Sarah and James meet and fall in love.

Stress in Word Groups

In certain types of word groups, one word will receive the primary stress, or emphasis. The following are some rules to help you determine where to place primary stress.

1. In noun phrases and prepositional phrases, the last noun usually gets primary stress.

    A. James Leads
    B. idealistic teacher
    C. in a school
    D. hearing-impaired students

2. When two nouns form a compound noun construction, the <u>first</u> noun gets primary stress.
    E. the hearing world

3. In verb phrases, the primary stress usually falls on the main verbs. Verb auxiliaries, modals, and the verb "be" do not usually get primary stress.
    F. thinks
    G. can teach

As You Watch the Movie

Directions: Read the following questions. Keep them in mind while you watch the movie. After the movie, discuss your answers to these questions with a small group of your classmates.

This movie introduces the viewer to the world of the deaf. As you watch, consider how different that world is from the world of hearing people. What symbols does the director use to show the world of silence? What symbols does the director use to show the world of sound? Consider what this movie says about the education of the handicapped. Who are the successful deaf in this movie? What are the attitudes of the different educators toward the issue of education for the hearing-impaired? What are the responses of the deaf to the type of education they receive? What are the attitudes of the parents in this movie toward their children's deafness?

Postmovie Discussion Questions

1. What problems do the deaf in the movie face in learning to communicate with hearing people?

2. What symbols does the director use to show the isolation of deafness?

3. What are some of the environmental differences between the school for the deaf and a school for hearing people?

4. How do the deaf indicate that they want someone's attention?

5. How do the deaf learn to dance?

6. What does Sarah initially give as her reason for not wanting to speak? What is her real reason for not wanting to speak? Is it because of the communication problem, or does she have another problem?

7. What is James's reaction to Johnny's refusal to speak and how does it compare to his reaction to Sarah's refusal to speak?

8. How does James make learning to speak a realistic, communicative activity for the students? What do you think of his methods? Which of his basic ideas about teaching communication would work in an ESL classroom?

9. As the movie progresses, how does Franklin's attitude toward Sarah and toward James change? Why does it change?

10. As the movie progresses, how does James's attitude change toward Sarah's refusal to speak? Why does he change?

11. How does Sarah's attitude change about herself? Why does it change?

12. What do you think Sarah will probably do at the end of the movie?

13. How does Sarah's mother's attitude change? Why does it change?

14. In what scenes does Sarah feel isolated from the world of the deaf?

15. In what scenes does Sarah feel isolated from the world of the hearing?

16. How does James try to understand how it feels to be deaf? Why does he try?

MOVIE REVIEW #1

Prereading

Directions: These are some of the words that you will need to understand before reading the passage.

" ":Quotation marks are <u>sometimes</u> used to indicate sarcasm or disbelief on the part of the writer.

> *Example:* Well, she's going to be very "happy" when she hears this news. (The writer does not believe that she will be happy.)

Vocabulary in Context

Directions: Read the following passage without using your dictionary. As you read the passage, try to guess the meaning of the following words, all of which are underlined in the passage. Write your guesses in the appropriate column and then look up the words in an English-English dictionary to check your guesses. Afterwards, reread the passage, using your dictionary, and do the exercises at the end of the passage.

Words	My Guess	Dictionary Definition
struggle		
challenges		
drifted		
landed		

<u>Words</u>	<u>My Guess</u>	<u>Dictionary Definition</u>
at the onset		
restless		
to make waves		
custodian		
bright		
janitorial		
traumatized		
adamantly		
rage		
sweep over		
eloquent		

Words	My Guess	Dictionary Definition
longs		
to draw		
delineation		
enigma		
overbearing		
poses		
threat		
crucial		

CHILDREN OF A LESSER GOD

by Kevin Thomas

From: Los Angeles Times, Friday, October 3, 1986.

1   "Children of a Lesser God" is an exceptionally adroit adaptation of a play onto the
2   screen. As a film, it flows beautifully under Randa Haines's direction and has considerable
3   humor as well as dramatic intensity. It is a classic love story—romantic, passionate,
4   involving, vibrant characters.
5   What makes it different is that the woman has been deaf her entire life. This means
6   that in this couple's <u>struggle</u> to communicate we see magnified the <u>challenges</u> that face any
7   two people attempting to make a life together in today's world. James (William Hurt) is a
8   teacher of speech to the hard of hearing, who's <u>drifted</u> from one school to the next until he
9   has <u>landed</u> on a quaint Victorian campus on the coast of Maine. <u>At the onset,</u> the decent
10 but conservative head of the school (Philip Bosco) tells this clearly <u>restless</u> man not <u>to make</u>
11 <u>waves.</u>
12   James soon has his eleventh-graders dancing to rock music, and they happily respond
13 to the vibrations. He has also noticed a beautiful young woman named Sarah (Marlee
14 Matlin, who actually is hard of hearing) once a pupil but now a <u>custodian.</u> He quickly
15 realizes that she's as <u>bright</u> as her temperament is fiery.
16   But why should she spend her life doing <u>janitorial</u> work? What <u>traumatized</u> her so
17 that she <u>adamantly</u> refuses to try to learn how to speak, preferring only to sign? (Ironically,
18 while in time we learn all about Sarah, we never know as much about James as we'd like to.)
19 What makes "Children of a Lesser God" come so poignantly alive is its understanding of
20 the psychology of close relationships between the hard of hearing and "normal" people.
21 Anyone who grew up with a parent or relative who was hard of hearing will recognize the
22 frustration and the <u>rage</u> that so frequently <u>sweep over</u> Sarah, making life difficult and
23 exhausting for James as well as for herself.
24   Sarah has turned signing into a kind of swift, <u>eloquent</u> form of expression, but for
25 James, signing sometimes becomes tiring. He <u>longs</u> to listen to his beloved Bach but how
26 can he enjoy such music when his lover can't?
27   At the same time we come to appreciate Sarah's need <u>to draw</u> reinforcement,
28 inspiration, and relaxation from being with others who are hearing-impaired—and that
29 this need applies to members of any minority.
30   Hurt and Matlin's finely drawn portrayals emerge from this painfully accurate
31 <u>delineation</u> of tensions underlying the relationship. James is so deeply in love and so
32 deeply challenged by the <u>enigma</u> that is Sarah that he is in danger of becoming more of an

33 overbearing invader than a lover. Sarah, in turn, is so fiercely proud and independent and
34 self-enclosed that she poses an equal threat to their relationship.
35   Hurt and Matlin make James and Sarah's passion for each other a tangible experi-
36 ence; the question is whether they'll stop struggling to bring each other into the other's
37 world long enough to discover how to create a world of their own. Crucial to their fate is
38 Sarah's mother, beautifully underplayed by Piper Laurie, as a woman whose bitter
39 indifference to her daughter proves deceptive.
40   Playwright Mark Medoff and his co-adapter Hesper Anderson have carefully re-
41 thought his stage piece as a movie. The result is a handsome film (rated R for blunt
42 language, signed and spoken, and some nudity) to which cinematographer John Seale
43 gives a mellow, burnished glow, complementing production designer Gene Callahan's
44 warm, traditional settings. Medoff does have a notion of what it takes to handle whatever
45 fate has dealt us.

Reading for Full Comprehension

1. On line 5, the writer says "What makes it different is . . . ." What is he
   referring to? In other words, what is it different from?

2. On line 29, what do the words "this need" refer to?

3. T/F   It is implied that the author of this article has one or more family
   members who are hard of hearing.

4. T/F   The author does not believe that deaf people are normal.

   One quick way to find out a reviewer's basic opinion is to read the first and
   last paragraphs and to find and mark the one, general, opinion sentence in
   each paragraph in the article. Put together, these will give you a pretty good
   idea of the opinion of the author. Since reviews tend to give plenty of
   examples from the movie, one easy way to find the opinion of the author is
   to look for a general sentence that has few, if any, specific examples from
   the movie.

5. Find and underline one general opinion sentence about the movie in the
   second paragraph.

6. Find and underline one general opinion sentence about the movie in the
   fourth paragraph.

7. Find and underline one general opinion sentence about the movie in the
   seventh paragraph.

8. Find and underline one general opinion sentence about the movie in the
   ninth paragraph.

9. Summarize this reading selection in 75 to 100 words.

MOVIE REVIEW #2

Vocabulary in Context

Directions: Read the following passage without using your dictionary. As you read the passage, try to guess the meaning of the following words, all of which are underlined in the passage. Write your guesses in the appropriate column and then look up the words in an English-English dictionary to check your guesses. Afterwards, reread the passage, using your dictionary, and do the exercises at the end of the passage.

Words	My Guess	Dictionary Definition
obsessed		
risks		
device		
imposes		
mark		
self-actualization		
barriers		

Words	My Guess	Dictionary Definition
trauma		
betrays		
precise		

DIRECTOR KEEPS WORLD OF THE DEAF AT ARM'S LENGTH

by Dave Kehr

1   . . . In "Children of a Lesser God," the film that director Randa Haines has made
2   from Mark Medoff's play, deafness is used as a metaphor for emotional withdrawal. The
3   film is about a speech teacher (William Hurt) who becomes <u>obsessed</u> with a young,
4   beautiful, and highly intelligent deaf woman (Marlee Matlin) who refuses to learn to use
5   her voice, preferring to communicate through sign language. As Hurt works with her, he
6   falls in love, but she continues to push him away. She wants to stay in her own private
7   world, safe from the <u>risks</u> of human contact.
8   There is a real subject here—the world of the deaf—and one that the movies, a
9   medium that has always emphasized the visual over the aural, seems uniquely qualified to
10 treat. But Haines's direction makes no attempt to enter that world, to show us how the deaf
11 perceive, feel, and act as unhearing people. Instead, she stays on the fringes, using Hurt as
12 an audience identification figure and keeping Matlin at arm's length.
13   Though Matlin and Hurt communicate through sign language, the movie has Hurt
14 provide a running translation into spoken English, a <u>device</u> that quickly becomes artificial
15 (Hurt has to keep telling his partner how she feels: "So you feel angry, do you?") and also
16 <u>imposes</u> an artificial distance between the character and the viewer. Because we are unable
17 to understand her language, she remains an exotic, remote, strange figure. The film,
18 inadvertently perhaps, implies that she is something other than human.
19   The use of subtitles would have bridged that gap in a minute, but Haines has her
20 reasons for preserving our separation from Matlin. Rather than make a film about

21 deafness, she has decided to squeeze the subject into the standard go-for-it formula:
22 Matlin's acquisition of spoken language will <u>mark</u> the fulfillment of her human potential—
23 she'll be "all that she can be" . . .
24   The formula demands that Matlin's road to <u>self-actualization</u> be filled with as many
25 <u>barriers</u> as possible, and the screenwriters have provided all they can imagine: an absent
26 father, a mother (Piper Laurie) who hates her for frightening the father away, a childhood
27 marked by sexual <u>trauma</u>. The film seems to be suggesting that deafness is not a physical
28 problem but a psychological one.
29   By turning the fact of deafness into a psychological metaphor, Haines <u>betrays</u> its
30 reality. The film turns into a stream of clichés ("You can do whatever you want!"), and
31 nothing in it has the weight of experience. For Haines, Matlin becomes "one of us"—fully
32 "human"—only when she emerges from the psychological shell her deafness has provided
33 and learns to return Hurt's affection. This is pure sentimentalism, and it does no service to
34 the hearing-impaired.
35   But there is one remarkable element in "Children of a Lesser God," and that is Marlee
36 Matlin's performance. An intense, burning presence, she is able to break through the
37 film's metaphoric vagueness and provide a glimpse of the genuine. Her signing—rapid,
38 graceful, nuanced—has an eloquence even for those who (like myself) do not understand
39 the <u>precise</u> meaning of the symbols she employs. The expressivity of her gestures recalls
40 the time when the movies themselves could not hear and made the very best of it—the 30
41 years of silent film.

Reading for Full Comprehension

1. To what do the words "a device" (line 14) refer?

2. To what do the words "that gap" (line 19) refer?

3. To what do the words "this" and "it" (line 33) refer?

4. T/F   The writer does not think that film is a good way to explore the world of the deaf.

5. T/F   The author thinks that it is a good idea that Matlin's character (Sarah) become like a hearing person.

6. T/F   The author does not approve of the use of the "go-for-it" formula.

7. In which paragraph, number 1 or number 2, does the author express his opinions about the movie?

8. Underline all the opinion words (adjectives), phrases, and sentences of the third paragraph.

9. Find a general opinion sentence in the fifth paragraph.

10. What is, in this author's opinion, the best point about the movie? Use your own words to answer this question.

11. Summarize this reading selection in 75 to 100 words.

WRITING ASSIGNMENTS

1. Write an essay in which you describe the history of handicapped education in the United States. Start with a paragraph in which you define handicaps. Then, develop a paragraph on the education of the handicapped in the nineteenth century, and give an example of one specific handicap. Add a paragraph on the education of the handicapped in the twentieth century. Write a final paragraph in which you describe the impact of P.L. 94-142 on handicapped education.

2. How does Sarah's life reflect the change in attitudes toward educating the handicapped in the United States? Write a paragraph in which you describe Sarah's life and another in which you show how it is reflective of the changes in the attitudes toward education of the handicapped.

3. Compare and contrast the education of the handicapped in 1889 with the education of the handicapped in 1989. Write two paragraphs, one in which you describe handicapped education in 1889 and one in which you contrast it with handicapped education in 1989. You might want to add one more paragraph in which you state your opinions about handicapped education now, and what you think the education of the handicapped will be like in the near future.

4. Pretend you are a hearing trustee of Gallaudet University. Write a letter to the editor of a Washington D.C. newspaper in which you defend the choice of a hearing person for president. Remember, some people will disagree with you. What will their objections be? Make sure you anticipate and address the counterarguments. Structure your letter as follows: an introduction containing both a thesis sentence introducing the issue and a sentence stating the counterarguments, a paragraph explaining why those opposed are wrong, and two or three paragraphs explaining why you are right.

5. Pretend you are a deaf student of Gallaudet University. Write a letter to the board of trustees explaining why you think a deaf president is needed. Remember, some people will disagree with you. What will their objections be? Make sure you anticipate and answer the objections. Structure your letter as follows: an introduction containing a thesis sentence, a sentence stating the opinions of those who disagree, a paragraph explaining why the opposition is wrong, and two or three paragraphs explaining why you are right.

6. You are the principal of a school with a few handicapped students. Interpret the process of P.L. 94-142 to a group of new teachers. Take the six

points listed in the article by Good and Brophy and develop a paragraph for each in which you explain what each point means for teachers.

7. Consider your classroom, building, and campus. What conveniences exist for the handicapped? Choose one of these settings and write a short guide for the handicapped on your campus, explaining what facilities exist, where they are located, and who could best benefit by using them. You might want to write a separate paragraph for each structural feature.

8. Find two structural features in your building, class, or campus that could be improved for the handicapped. Write a letter to your student paper in which you argue for the incorporation of these features. Explain the changes that need to be made, where they need to be made, and whom they would benefit.

9. How are the handicapped educated in your country? Write an essay describing what you know of this education and compare it with what you know of the education of the handicapped in the United States. Start with a paragraph in which you describe handicapped education in one country and write another paragraph in which you compare it with handicapped education in the other country.

10. Interview a handicapped person. Ask him or her what two or three things he or she would like to see changed to make life easier for the handicapped. Write a report explaining these changes. In your introduction, describe him or her and his or her handicap and write a thesis sentence in which you indicate his or her suggestions for the changes. Take each change and write a separate paragraph for it.

11. Describe the attitude of most people in your country toward the handicapped. What special facilities exist in your country for the handicapped? How or what could your country change to make life easier for the handicapped? Write an introduction in which you describe the attitudes and facilities. In a thesis sentence, state your opinion about what improvements could be made. Develop your reasons in two or three separate paragraphs.

3

WHOSE LAND IS IT ANYWAY?

A. What are these people doing?

B. Do certain groups of people in your country do this type of work?

C. Who do you think these people are?

INTRODUCTION

Directions: Read the following passage without using your dictionary. Do the exercises after the passage.

1   People are often surprised to learn that some of the territory of the United States is
2 still under dispute. In the past decade, news stories have told of Indian tribes fighting
3 (usually in the courts) with the government of the United States for fishing or hunting
4 rights on government-owned land. However, most Americans know that the original
5 European colonizers of America bought, stole, and forcibly took the land of the country
6 away from the Indians (also called the Native Americans). That the Indians should be
7 disputing land claims with the government is hardly surprising.
8   The Native Americans aren't, however, the only ones who are angry with the
9 government of the United States about land that was taken away from them. The
10 Chicanos, the Spanish-speaking people of the Southwest, also have disputes with
11 the government about the land. The basis for their disputes with the government, like
12 those of the Indians, is historical. Before the United States and Mexico signed the Treaty
13 of Guadalupe Hidalgo in 1848, much of the land of the Southwest belonged to Mexico.
14 The treaty, however, ended the Mexican War by establishing the present border between
15 the United States and Mexico, giving much of the land of the Southwest to the United
16 States. The area's Spanish-speaking inhabitants thus became citizens of the United States.
17   Since the signing of the treaty, the Chicanos have preserved the idea that the
18 Southwest is their lost land. Periodically, over the past century and one-half, arguments
19 have arisen between Chicanos and Anglo-Americans over possession and use of lands in
20 the Southwest. As you will see in this chapter, some of these small arguments, on occasion,
21 threaten to become small wars.

Reading for Full Comprehension

One way writers explain a new term is to give a definition of the term immediately after the term. This type of definition is usually preceded and followed by commas. Sometimes, the words of the actual definition are preceded by such words as "that is" or "or."

Examples: The settlers, or first inhabitants of the place, decided to stay.

The settlers, that is the first inhabitants of the place, decided to stay.

The settlers, the first inhabitants of the place, decided to stay.

1.   What is the author's definition of the word "Chicanos"?

2.   Which countries fought in the Mexican War?

3. Which country won the Mexican War?

4. List the three results of the Treaty of Guadalupe Hidalgo.

5. Give another word from this passage that means the same as "fighting."

READING #1

Vocabulary in Context

Directions: Read the following passage without using your dictionary. As you read the passage, try to guess the meaning of the following words, all of which have been underlined in the passage. Write your guesses in the appropriate column and when you have finished reading, look up the words in an English-English dictionary to check your guesses. Then reread the passage, using your dictionary, and do the exercises at the end of the passage.

<u>Words</u>	<u>My Guess</u>	<u>Dictionary Definition</u>
descent		
indigenous to		
designations		

As you have learned in previous chapters, the Latin root "pater" means "father." An alternate spelling of this root is "patr-." What do you think the word "patrimony" means?

"Dis" is a prefix which can mean "removed from." A disoriented person is one who is removed from his or her sense of orientation. A dislocated person is one who is removed from his or her location. What do you think the words "dispossessed of" mean?

THE CHICANO IMAGE OF THE SOUTHWEST

by John R. Chavez

Condensed from: John R. Chavez, The Lost Land: The Chicano Image of the Southwest (Albuquerque: University of New Mexico Press, 1984).

1   To the Chicanos, the Spanish-surnamed population of the Southwest, the image of
2 the Southwest is clear. The Southwest—a land including California, Arizona, New
3 Mexico, Texas, and Colorado—is where 85 percent of U.S. citizens of Mexican descent
4 reside. To the Chicanos, it is their homeland, their lost homeland, the conquered northern
5 half of the Mexican nation.
6   Before the war between the United States and Mexico, which ended in 1848, present-
7 day California, Texas, Nevada, Utah, Arizona, New Mexico, more than half of Colorado,
8 the Oklahoma Panhandle, and parts of Wyoming and Kansas were all parts of Mexico's
9 national territory. To Chicanos, this territory remains their patrimony although they
10 inhabit in significant numbers only five of the states mentioned. Chicanos consider
11 themselves indigenous to the region. Their claims are supported by the fact that their
12 ancestors not only explored and settled parts of the Southwest as early as the sixteenth
13 century, but thousands of years earlier permanently occupied the region or migrated
14 through it on their way south. The belief that the Southwest is the Chicano homeland and
15 the belief that Mexicans are indigenous to and dispossessed of the region are beliefs that
16 have had a formative and continuing influence on the collective Chicano mind.
17   There are substantial differences between the Anglo-American view of the Southwest
18 and that of the Chicanos. First of course, is the Anglos' image of the West as vacant before
19 the arrival of the Anglos; Chicanos can hardly accept this since their predecessors had
20 already founded such cities as San Antonio, Santa Fe, Tucson, and Los Angeles well
21 before the appearance of Anglo-Americans. Second, such regional designations as "Far
22 West" and, of course, "Southwest" itself are applied from the perspective of the Anglo-
23 American cultural centers on the Atlantic seaboard. These designations certainly do not
24 correspond to the Chicano picture, since Chicanos view their region from the perspective
25 of their cultural center in Mexico City. Furthermore, the current of their history has
26 flowed south and north, not east and west.
27   As a result of this perspective, Chicanos view the Southwest as an extension of Mexico
28 and Latin America, a Mexican region spreading beyond what is regarded as an artificial
29 international boundary. Geographically, in fact, the Southwest does resemble the Mexican
30 deserts and highlands more closely than it does the plains and woodlands of the eastern
31 United States.

32 The Chicano myth, however, does bear important similarities to the Native American
33 image of the United States. Both Indians and Chicanos see themselves as indigenous to
34 and dispossessed of their homelands, which in the Southwest means they claim the same
35 territory. Nevertheless, in the twentieth century these overlapping claims have caused
36 little conflict, for Anglos have simply possessed the land; instead these claims have led the
37 two minorities to recognize that they have common backgrounds.

38 Unlike Mexican nationals, the Chicanos see the Southwest more readily than Mexico
39 as their homeland, and consequently picture themselves more readily as a people of that
40 region than of Mexico. While Mexico remains the homeland in the sense of a mother-
41 land—a cultural source and a nation of origin—the Southwest is the present home of
42 Chicanos, a home that since 1848 has helped make them what they are.

43 Over the last 140 years, the myth of the lost land has served as a focus for Mexican
44 nationalism in the Southwest. The myth has more often roused the pride of Southwest
45 Mexicans, reminding them of their long history in and prior rights to the region. Indeed,
46 these rights have formed the foundation for claims of many kinds against United States
47 society. Over the decades, the region's Mexicans have defended their language, customs,
48 property, freedom of movement, and their very dignity on the basis of their rights as a
49 native people, as well as their rights as citizens. There exists a recurring hope for the
50 recovery of that territory in one form or another. In the late 1960s this deep wish
51 reappeared in repeated Chicano allusions to the ancient Aztec homeland of Aztlan,
52 traditionally located in the Southwest.

53 The desire of Southwest Mexicans for recovery of the region has always been tied to
54 their desire for cultural, political, and economic self-determination, a self-determination
55 they believe can only be achieved through control of the space they occupy. The story of
56 the struggle for that environment is central to Chicano history.

Reading for Full Comprehension

1. Metaphor is a form of comparison. In metaphor, the writer makes the
    comparison by referring to someone or something as something else. For
    example, a writer might choose to refer to a very hungry person as an
    attacker and a table of food as a battlefield.

    Example: He assaulted the table with a merciless fury, laying waste to the
            elegantly piled dishes.

    Verbs, adjectives, and adverbs most often are used to create a metaphor. If
    you check the underlined words in your dictionary, you will find these
    words are most often used to describe battles. The writer is comparing the
    hungry man's eating of the food to an attacker doing battle.
    Look at the sentence on lines 25 and 26, "Furthermore, the current. . . ."
    Look up the words "current" and "flowed" in your dictionary. In this
    sentence, the author compares history to a _____.

2. Another technique of writers is to use synonyms instead of repeating words
    in a text. In this text, the author uses many different words to repeat the idea

of ". . . beliefs that have had . . ." on lines 15 and 16. Look at lines 27, 32, and 39. What nouns and verbs does the author use to express the idea of "belief"? List the words:

What is another word in the same paragraph for "the perspective" on line 22?

3. What do the words "their claims" on line 11 refer to?

4. How does that author define the word "Chicanos"?

How is the definition different from the definition given in the Introduction?

5. How does the author define the words "the Southwest"?

6. To what do the words "this perspective" on line 27 refer?

7. To what do the words "that environment" on line 56 refer?

8. If the very first Spanish people went to the Southwest in the sixteenth century, is it correct to assume that the Chicanos are only of Spanish descent? Explain your answer by referring to the text.

9. What is the "artificial international boundary" mentioned on lines 28 and 29?

10. T/F   There are probably fewer Chicanos in Utah than in Colorado.

11. T/F   85 percent of the inhabitants of the Southwest are Chicano.

12. T/F   The author suggests that most Anglos understand the facts and dates of Chicano history.

13. T/F   The term "Southwest" shows the Anglo idea of the Southwest.

14. T/F   There are three important similarities between Chicano and Native American ideas of the Southwest.

15. T/F   Chicanos probably do not consider themselves citizens of the United States.

16. T/F   At times in the past, Native Americans and Chicanos probably have had disputes over the Southwest.

17. Summarize this reading selection in 75 to 100 words.

READING #2

Prereading

Directions: These are some words that you will need to understand before reading the passage.

National Guard: the state militia (self-defense army).

to be caught in a web (verbal idiom): to be trapped.

to go on welfare (verbal idiom): to receive basic financial help from the state/ federal government.

Vocabulary in Context

Directions: Read the following passage without using your dictionary. As you read the passage, try to guess the meaning of the following words, all of which have been underlined in the passage. Write your guesses in the appropriate column and when you have finished reading, look up the words in an English-English dictionary to check your guesses. Then reread the passage, using your dictionary, and do the exercises at the end of the passage.

Words	My Guess	Dictionary Definition
absorbed		
confiscated		
denounced		
spurt		
flocked		

GUERILLAS OF RIO ARRIBA: THE NEW MEXICAN LAND WARS

by Clark Knowlton

From: Clark Knowlton, "Guerillas of Rio Arriba," *The Nation* magazine, The Nation Co., Inc., 1968.

1   In 1847, the Spanish Americans were <u>absorbed</u> into the United States by military
2   conquest and against their will. The Spanish Americans were treated as a conquered
3   people by the incoming Anglos. Abandoned by both the American and Mexican govern-
4   ments, the rural, illiterate, Spanish-speaking village people, with little knowledge of
5   American laws and customs, were left to the contemptuous mercy of the ruthless,
6   dynamic, materialistic, individualistic frontier culture.
7   State and federal agencies <u>confiscated</u> large areas of their lands without compensa-
8   tion. The Spanish Americans were caught in the web of unfamiliar political, economic,
9   and judicial systems. One authority estimates that the Spanish Americans from the 1880s
10 to the 1930s lost more than 2 million acres of private lands and 1.7 million acres of
11 communal lands to private holders, 1.8 million acres to the state government, and an even
12 vaster but uncounted acreage to the federal government.
13   The fires of discontent have always burned in the northern mountains of New
14 Mexico. The anger flares up in an epidemic of fence cutting, barn and ranch-house
15 burnings, and warnings to the Anglo-American ranchers and politicians to vacate
16 Spanish-American lands. Cries for law and order bring out the troops and the National
17 Guard. Numerous Spanish Americans are jailed, their protest organizations are re-
18 pressed, their leaders are exiled, assassinated, or imprisoned. The Anglo-Americans
19 forget, but a new Spanish-American generation appears; new causes of protest arise; new
20 protest organizations develop. The cycle starts all over again.
21   Anger, bitterness, and resentment are blazing hot today. State officials armed with
22 writs are traveling from village to village requiring that villagers prove their title to the
23 irrigation water they use. Centuries-old Spanish-American customs of water use and
24 ownership are being disregarded. The villagers are convinced that they are to lose their
25 water as they lost their land. Spanish-American grazing rights in the national forests have
26 been sharply reduced in the past two or three years. Hundreds of small farming and
27 ranching families are faced with their emigrating to the urban slums or going on welfare.
28   The breaking point came suddenly in 1967. Thirteen fires were deliberately set that
29 summer in the national forests. Meetings took place in most of the villages. The local
30 people bitterly <u>denounced</u> the closing of village schools, the lack of roads, malnutrition,
31 loss of land and water, discrimination, erosion of grazing rights, and the failure of state or

32 federal government agencies to pay attention to Spanish-American needs and aspirations.
33 The Alianza Federal de Mercedes—the Federal Alliance of Land Grantees, now known as
34 the Alliance of Free City States—is the largest, the fastest growing, the most vigorous, and
35 the most important of a number of Spanish-American protest organizations. Its meetings
36 from 1963 to 1965 were attended largely by the rural poor, elderly Spanish Americans
37 who still had hopes of recovering the lands taken from them.
38   In 1966, its membership began to <u>spurt.</u> Alianza organizers became active in most of
39 the villages. Young people and veterans began to attend its meetings. Rural poor and
40 urban poor <u>flocked</u> into its ranks. The message of the Alianza was simple and to the point:
41 "You have been robbed of your lands, your water rights, your grazing rights, your
42 language and your culture. Together, we will get the land back—preferably through the
43 courts or Congress, but one way or another we will get it back."

Reading for Full Comprehension

1. What metaphor does the author use to describe the anger of the Spanish-Americans?

   What words does he use to make the comparison?

2. Look up the adjectives in the sentence "Abandoned by . . ." on line 3. Which group, the Spanish Americans or the Anglos, does the author seem to sympathize with?

3. List the steps in the "cycle" referred to on line 20.

4. What are the implications of Alianza's message ". . . preferably through the courts or Congress"? Does this mean the Alianza might be willing to support illegal actions to get the land back? Explain your answer.

5. T/F   The government has paid the Chicanos for the land that it took from them.

6. T/F   This article was probably written around 1967.

7. T/F   Chicanos are only concerned about land and irrigation problems.

8. T/F   Alianza was a stronger organization before 1966.

9. List some of the ways that Spanish Americans make money. Do they probably do more crop or animal farming?

10. Summarize this reading selection in 75 to 100 words.

READING #3

Prereading

Directions: These are some words that you will need to understand before reading the passage.

band-aid solution (compound noun): a temporary, usually ineffective solution to a problem.

high noon (noun phrase): a serious time, at which a critical decision must be made or action must be taken.

to have a hidden agenda (verbal idiom): to have a secret plan or purpose.
Example: His hidden agenda in requesting a transfer to New York was to be near his girlfriend.

moot question (noun phrase): a question without an answer. An irrelevant question.

Mother Nature (noun phrase): a popular way of saying "nature." It makes nature more personal.

to set a precedent (verbal idiom): to be the first in a series of similar events.
Example: His idea to have a Christmas party at the office set a precedent. Every year thereafter, they had a Christmas party at the office.

Vocabulary in Context

Directions: Read the following passage without using your dictionary. As you read the passage, try to guess the meaning of the following words, all of which have been underlined in the passage. Write your guesses in the appropriate column and when you have finished reading look up the words in an English-English dictionary to check your guesses. Then reread the passage, using your dictionary and do the exercises at the end of the passage.

Words	My Guess	Dictionary Definition

elk

access

Words	My Guess	Dictionary Definition

revenues

flock

opponents

A LAND BATTLE IN NEW MEXICO
The Milagro Sheep War

by James N. Baker with Peter Annin

From: Newsweek, September 19, 1989, © Newsweek, Inc. All rights reserved. Reprinted with permission.

1 It was high noon for the sheepherders. After a grazing lease with an Apache
2 reservation ran out late last month, desperate members of a Hispanic wool cooperative
3 decided to break the law and moved 2,000 sheep into a state-owned wildlife area near Los
4 Ojos in northern New Mexico. Prominent Anglo ranchers protested: the sheep would
5 compete with elk for the grazing land, they said, cutting into the cash big-game hunters
6 brought to the local economy every year. Gov. Garrey Carruthers sent in mounted rangers
7 to round up the "trespassers." In a compromise, he granted the sheepherders temporary
8 access to 800 acres of nearby Heron Lake State Park. Last week, time was running out on
9 the Band-Aid solution—and no one knew where the sheep would go next.
10 From the start, money has been at the center of the dispute. The shepherds belong to
11 Ganados del Valle (Livestock of the Valley), a flourishing co-op of 50 Hispanic families
12 started in 1983. Ganados raises churros, long-fleeced Spanish sheep first imported in the
13 16th century, and makes clothes and wall hangings to sell to tourists. (Expected revenues
14 this year: about $200,000.) If they find no grazing land, co-op leaders say, they will have to
15 sell or slaughter part of the flock. Opponents argue that elk hunters pour more money
16 into the economy, and that allowing Ganados to graze on the reserve would set a precedent
17 since other ranchers might demand access to state land, too.

18 How much harm could the sheep do? Ganados leaders cite environmental studies
19 claiming the animals would be helpful. "Vegetation needs something to recycle it, and
20 grazing has been shown as a good way to do that," says Karl Hess, a specialist with the New
21 Mexico Department of Agriculture. But an official at the state Department of Game and
22 Fish claims there are studies showing the opposite. The ranchers believe Mother Nature
23 has already made the whole question moot. A spring drought made vegetation sparse—
24 and all the more critical for the elk.
25 The most emotional source of the conflict has deep historic roots. Before New Mexico
26 became a U.S. territory in 1850, the Mexican government deeded Hispanic settlers in the
27 area a large communal land grant. In 1860, the United States permitted the land to fall
28 into the hands of one family, which was free to sell it off. Over the years, Anglos bought up
29 thousands of acres, making descendants of the original settlers bitter. As recently as 1967,
30 armed activists demanded the return of 2,500 square miles under old grants, forcing
31 authorities to call in the National Guard. Since then Anglo ranchers have been troubled by
32 barn burnings and fence cuttings. Some believe the co-op has a hidden agenda: "What
33 Ganados is after," says rancher Jim Mundy, "is the entire 500,000 acres of [the] land
34 grant." But Ganados leaders insist they have no link to the land-rights activists.
35 The governor has given a task force 30 days to study whether sheep grazing would be
36 good for the wildlife area. "I'm cautiously optimistic," says Ganados cofounder and
37 spokeswoman Maria Varela. Whatever the outcome, New Mexicans on both sides of the
38 battle have reason to hope for a lasting peace. Says Antonio Manzanares, chairman of
39 Ganados, "We're neighbors, whether we like it or not."

Reading for Full Comprehension

1. Where are the three places the sheep have grazed?
    a.
    b.
    c.

2. The word "Some" on line 32 refers to _____.

3. T/F   The writer of this piece probably agrees that the members of Ganados
    del Valle trespassed on federal land.

4. T/F   Some of the Anglos near Los Ojos do not trust the Chicanos.

5. Explain how the Hispanics in the area lost their land to the Anglos.

6. Summarize this reading selection in 75 to 100 words.

THE MOVIE: THE MILAGRO BEANFIELD WAR

Photofest

A. Who do you think these people are?

B. What do you think they are doing?

C. What part of the U.S. do you think they come from?

About the Movie

Directions: Divide the following reading into phrases. Determine where primary stress should fall in word groups. Practice reading the passage aloud. Following the instructions at the end of the passage, locate the primary sentence stress in each sentence. Reread the passage and discuss it with a classmate.

The Milagro Beanfield War takes place in a small town in New Mexico. The town, Milagro, is dying. Most of the Chicano inhabitants have left. A few, however, remain. There is the Mondragon family, Nancy, and José and their three children. José Mondragon works, when he can find work, as a repairman and a day laborer. There is a sheriff, Berney, José's cousin, who doesn't have much to do. José's father is dead, but he often comes back from the dead to talk to his friend Amarante Cordova, the retired mayor of the town. There is a woman mechanic, Ruby Archuleta, who is quite unhappy about the fact that the town is dying. She has an Anglo friend, a lawyer named Charley Bloom, who was once an activist for the Chicano cause. There is another Anglo, a sociologist from New York University named Herbert Platz, who is living with the Mondragons so that he can study the culture of the region.

There is also some possible change in Milagro's future. An Anglo developer, Mr. Devine, of the Devine Land and Cattle Company, wants to turn the area into the Miracle Valley Recreation Area. Mr. Devine controls the irrigation system around Milagro. He can buy the land cheaply as soon as it has dried up. One day, José Mondragon accidentally kicks a lock on one of Mr. Devine's irrigation ditches. Water from the ditch spills into an old dried out beanfield that was owned by José's father. José decides to take advantage of the accident and plants beans. The Devine Land and Cattle Company is upset that José is using Devine's water. Mr. Devine takes his problem to the state government. The state has deliberately dried up the area and raised taxes to encourage the Chicano farmers to sell to developers. The state doesn't want José to use the water to irrigate the land, but at the same time it doesn't want the Chicanos in the area to realize what the state has done to them. The solution would appear to be a Mr. Montana, who promises the state and Mr. Devine that he will take care of the situation without any publicity.

But the state hasn't counted on the fact that some of the Chicanos are already aware of what the state and Mr. Devine are trying to do. In fact, Ruby, the mechanic, is ready to start holding town meetings and circulate a petition.

It looks as if the little accident that watered the beanfield may start a war.

Sentence Stress

In addition to a primary stress in word groups, each sentence has a primary stress that is stronger than any other stress in the sentence.

To locate the primary sentence stress in each sentence, you must first divide each sentence into phrases. Then, remove unstressed function words from the phrases:

prepositions, auxiliary verbs, pronouns, and articles. The remaining words are called content words, which are usually stressed.

For example, take the first sentence:

| NP | VP | PP | PP |
The Milagro Beanfield War I takes place I in a small town I in New Mexico.

Next, place stress on word groups:

Milagro Beanfield War   takes place   small town   New Mexico.

Finally, the primary sentence stress usually falls on the last content word in the last phrase of the sentence:

The Milagro Beanfield War takes place in a small town in New Mexico.

Cultural Points about the Movie

Directions: Read the following passage and discuss the questions at the end of the passage with a small group of your classmates.

Ninety percent of Hispanic Americans are Roman Catholics. Since Roman Catholicism was first introduced to Latin America by the Spanish colonizers, it has changed greatly. Today, there are several differences in the practices and beliefs of Latin-American Catholics that do not exist in the practices and beliefs of Catholics in other parts of the world.

Belief in the helping power of saints is an integral part of Roman Catholicism everywhere; but in Latin America, especially in the small villages, the saints, called "los santos" have very special importance. Many Latin Americans, like Catholics everywhere, have their favorite saints, whom they pray to in times of trouble. A favorite saint of many people is Saint Jude, who is often called the patron saint of desperate causes. It is not uncommon to hear people in trouble remark that they will "say a prayer to Saint Jude" for help. In Latin America, such prayers are often said at little shrines, called "capillas," located in churches and homes. It is also common to see votive candles burning in front of statues of saints located in these little shrines.

All faithful Catholics believe in a life after death. Most, however, believe that this life and the life after death (often called the "afterlife") are separate. Latin-American Catholics, on the other hand, have a strong sense of the continuity of the life spectrum. For many Latin Americans, especially rural villagers, there is not a clear division between the two lives. It is not uncommon to hear Latin-American peasants say that they were just "talking to" a person who is dead. Nor is it uncommon for Latin-American Catholics to believe that a dead person can influence the course of events in this life. In small villages, one can often find people who believe that the dead walk among the living. This latter belief is particularly strong in rural Mexico. In fact, the great Mexican novelist Juan Rulfo wrote extensively about this belief in many of his works, including his most famous book *Pedro Paramo*. Other Latin-American authors, such as Gabriel Garcia-Marquez of Colombia, have also written about these beliefs.

— — — — —

One popular form of public protest in the United States is the circulation of petitions. A petition is a letter, usually addressed to a government official, that either makes a complaint or requests a specific action to be taken. The petition is usually signed by a large number of people.

Discussion Questions

1. Discuss the ways in which people pray in a religion you are familiar with. How are they similar to or different from the ways discussed in this passage?

2. Do (groups of) people in your country believe in ghosts? If so, what do they believe about them?

3. How do people in your country complain to the government?

As You Watch the Movie

Directions: Read the following questions. Keep them in mind while you watch the movie. After the movie, discuss your answers to these questions with a small group of your classmates.

This is a movie about a small New Mexican land war. As you watch the movie, consider the reasons each person gives for the action he or she takes. What are Mr. Devine's reasons? What are José Mondragon's reasons? As the characters change, how do their reasons change? Also, consider what the characters know and assume about each other.

Postmovie Discussion Questions

1. What were José Mondragon's reasons for watering the beanfield?

2. What were Mr. Devine's reasons for developing the Miracle Valley Recreation Area?

3. How did the different people in Milagro react to the beanfield—Ruby, Charley, the sheriff, Nancy Mondragon? What were their reasons for taking the actions that they did?

4. What does the sociologist learn about Mexican-American culture?

5. What are some examples of discrimination against Mexican Americans in this movie?

6. What is the purpose of the angel in the movie? How do the dead influence the living?

7. What significance does the town's name have? (Remember: milagro means "miracle" in Spanish.)

MOVIE REVIEW #1

Prereading

Directions: These are some of the words that you will need to understand before reading the passage.

60s activist (compound noun): someone who was politically involved in the civil rights movement or the anti-Vietnam war demonstrations of the 1960s.

back-to-the-earth (adj.): glorifying the earth and those people who work the earth.
  Example: Many young people in the 1960s joined the back-to-the-earth movement and went to live on farms.

El gringo supremo: the supreme North American. "Gringo" is a word used by Hispanics to refer to non-Hispanic North Americans. Sometimes it has a friendly meaning; at other times it has a negative meaning.

feel-good (adj.): something that makes someone feel good about himself/herself.

[to] get off the ground (verbal idiom): to begin something successfully.

Gone with the Wind: a very successful movie that cost a lot of money to produce.

gung-ho (adj.): enthusiastic, hard-working.
  Example: Her gung-ho spirit encouraged her co-workers.

hard to swallow (adj.): not believable.

Heaven's Gate: a very unsuccessful movie that cost a lot of money to produce.

muscle (noun): a person or persons who do(es) physical work for (an)other person(s). This physical work usually involves bodyguard-type work.
  Example: The rock band hired a motorcycle gang as muscle at their last concert.

right off the bat (adv.): at the very beginning.

the first order of business (noun phrase): the first thing to do before anything
    else.

Vocabulary in Context

*Directions: Read the following passage without using your dictionary. As you read
    the passage, try to guess the meaning of the following words, all of which
    have been underlined in the passage. Write your guesses in the appropri-
    ate column and when you have finished reading, look up the words in an
    English-English dictionary to check your guesses. Then reread the pas-
    sage, using your dictionary, and do the exercises at the end of the
    passage.*

Words	My Guess	Dictionary Definition
speculation		
flourishing		
connivers		

"Col" is a prefix that can mean "together." "Labor" is a root meaning "work." What
is a "collaboration?"

"Pre" is a prefix that means "before." "Concep" is a root meaning "idea." What is a
"preconception?"

TROUBLE IN MIRACLE VALLEY
Robert Redford makes
a feel-good fable

by David Ansen with Michael Reese

From: Newsweek, March 28, 1988, © Newsweek, Inc. All rights reserved. Reprinted
by permission.

1   It's been eight years since Robert Redford directed his Oscar-winning "Ordinary
2 People." For someone under the intense scrutiny of the media, rumors and speculation

3 inevitably arose. Why did his next movie take so long to get off the ground? Why was it
4 taking forever to shoot? It must be in trouble or he wouldn't be buried endlessly in the
5 editing room. And wasn't there something odd about a blond-haired, blue-eyed superstar
6 —el gringo supremo—making a movie whose heart and soul was Hispanic? Was "The
7 Milagro Beanfield War" going to be Redford's "Gone with the Wind"—or his "Heaven's
8 Gate"?

9   Now that it has arrived, the first order of business is to forget all your preconceptions.
10 Nothing Redford has done before will prepare you for the essentially modest, wide-eyed
11 charm of this crowded cinematic fable. Imagine a combination of Frank Capra's feel-good
12 sentimentality, a touch of the gung-ho communal spirit of King Vidor's 1934 back-to-the-
13 earth classic "Our Daily Bread" and a liberal sprinkling of Gabriel Garcia Marquez's
14 magical realism and you'll have a hint of what Redford is up to in his sweet-natured
15 adaptation of John Nichols's sprawling New Mexican novel. "The Milagro Beanfield War"
16 is a populist pipe dream of a movie, old-fashioned in its utter lack of cynicism and its
17 wishful, team-spirit politics, and very up to date in its sly, underplayed texture and jumpy
18 rhythms. Anyone allergic to whimsy in any form should beware; for the rest of us,
19 "Milagro" provides plenty to smile about.

20   Redford lets us know right off the bat that realism will take a back seat to the fabulist.
21 An old man, Amarante Cordova (Carlos Riquelme), is visited by an "angel" (Roberto
22 Carricart) who warns him that his town, Milagro, is dying. The immediate threat is the
23 Miracle Valley Recreation Area, a land-development project which will bring in golf
24 courses and hotels—and higher taxes, which will in turn drive the local population off the
25 land they've worked for generations. What sparks the "war" between the developer
26 (Richard Bradford) and the community is a small spontaneous act of defiance. Joe
27 Mondragon (Chick Vennera) kicks a water pipe and diverts the flow of the corporation's
28 water onto his family's field. His beanfield—improbably flourishing in the dry New
29 Mexico landscape—becomes the symbol around which his fellow Milagrans will come
30 together in open revolt.

31 **Scene-stealing pig:** Morally, the issue is cut and dried. Redford's developers, in
32 cahoots with the governor, are profit-hungry connivers with no concern for the culture
33 they will thoughtlessly displace, and they have no compunction about sending in outside
34 muscle (villainous Christopher Walken) to see that things go their way. The good guys of
35 Milagro are at odds with each other about the impact of Miracle Valley. Redford makes the
36 community his collective hero, and he's very adept at sketching his huge cast of characters
37 in quick, pungent strokes. A wonderful actor's director, he gets a superb performance
38 from the veteran Mexican star Riquelme, an actor so crafty he can steal scenes from his
39 constant companion, a scene-stealing pig. Ruben Blades is wonderfully droll as the town's
40 paunchy, slow-moving sheriff, and just as good are Daniel Stern as the comical sociology
41 student from NYU trying to grasp the often mystical rites of the townsfolk and John
42 Heard as a former '60s activist bullied against his will into rekindling his old radical fires.
43 There's fine work also from Chick Vennera as Mondragon, Julie Carmen as his passionate
44 wife, the eerily evil Walken and crusty James Gammon as the one member of the
45 establishment side with a divided heart. Sonia Braga has perhaps the most idealized, and
46 difficult, role as the fiery activist Ruby, a rather improbable feminist icon who is a bit hard
47 to swallow even in the context of a fable.

48   Redford, working from a script by David Ward and Nichols, keeps so many charac-
49   ters, events, and wry details spinning in the air that one is willing to forgive his occasional
50   lapses. That skipping, accordion-playing angel gets mighty precious at times; more
51   seriously, the crucial issue of the water rights is set up so sketchily you don't know what
52   exactly is at stake when Mondragon starts his beanfield. But in the face of "Milagro's"
53   balmy comic glow, you may find your jaded defenses melting. Perhaps it's the exquisite
54   New Mexican light, beautifully captured by cinematographer Robbie Greenberg, which
55   makes this fable so ultimately seductive. "The Milagro Beanfield War" gives off the
56   honeyed glow of wishful thinking. Even the violence that shockingly bursts out proves to
57   be nonlethal, and characters on the brink of death come back to life. Wouldn't it be nice,
58   Redford is asking, if the world worked this way? And for two hours at least, he playfully
59   charms us into thinking it could be so.
60   Redford had no cinematic model in mind for "Milagro." But there were certain
61   writers whose magical tone he aspired to: he mentions Isaac Bashevis Singer and Garcia
62   Marquez.
63   Ruben Blades, the Panamanian salsa singer and Harvard law-school graduate turned
64   actor, sees the crosscultural experience [of this movie] as a positive one. "No doubt there's
65   a need for Latinos to write screenplays and for Latinos to direct," he says. "But we should
66   try to establish collaborations with the Anglo representatives of the arts. Redford made it
67   possible for non-Anglo actors to have a good script, characters that weren't negative, and,
68   most important, to have the opportunity to work and collaborate. With this movie he
69   proves that hearts don't require visas and emotions don't require subtitles." Actor Stern
70   puts it more bluntly: "Let's face it, if 'Milagro' had been directed by a Chicano director, it
71   would not have been made. It needed a champion—not because it was a Chicano story but
72   because of the smallness of it. It was a hard sell." What everyone seems to forget in the
73   argument about a gringo directing Latinos is that "Milagro" was always a crossover
74   project: it was written by a gringo in the first place, albeit one deeply familiar with the
75   territory.

Reading for Full Comprehension

1. The words "a touch of" and "a liberal sprinkling of" in the sentence, "Imagine a . . ." on lines 11–15 are often used in recipes. In this sentence the author compares the movie to a _____.

2. Look up the words "sketching" and "strokes" in the sentence, "Redford makes . . ." on lines 35–37. In this sentence the author compares the director to a _____.

3. T/F   The author would agree that *Milagro Beanfield War* is Redford's *Heaven's Gate.*

4. T/F   Actor Blades thinks it would have been better to have a Latin director direct this movie.

5. T/F   Actor Stern doesn't think a Chicano would do a good job of directing this movie.

6. How does the author define a crossover project on line 73? What punctuation does he use to give his example?

7. On line 11, the reviewer calls this movie a "cinematic fable." He then goes on, in later parts of the review, to explain the comparison to a fable. What elements of the movie are like those of a fable according to the author?

8. In movie reviews, the authors usually comment on several different parts of the movie, including the actors, the visual effects, the story of the movie, and the music. As you reread this review, fill in the following chart.

OPINION	GOOD	BAD	NO OPINION	SPECIFIC COMMENTS
Cast in general				
actor 1 Ruben Blades	X			wonderfully droll
actor 2				
actor 3				
actor 4				
actor 5				
actor 6				
actor 7				
Visual effects				
Story of the movie				
Music				

9. Summarize this reading selection in 75 to 100 words.

Movie Review #2

Prereading

Directions: These are some of the words you will need to understand before reading the passage.

a piece of work (noun phrase): a difficult or unusual person.

white-bread (adj.): plain and uninteresting.

-ville: this is a suffix used to mean "in a place where things are typical of x." For example, if a reviewer said that "this movie is a classic work from Redfordville," it would mean "from the work of Redford."

Vocabulary in Context

Directions: Read the following passage without using your dictionary. As you read the passage, try to guess the meaning of the following words, all of which have been underlined in the passage. Write your guesses in the appropriate column and when you have finished reading, look up the words in an English-English dictionary to check your guesses. Then reread the passage, using your dictionary, and do the exercises at the end of the passage.

Words	My Guess	Dictionary Definition
visitations		
hub		
warily		
charting		

'MILAGRO' MAGIC RELIES ON REDFORD'S WARM TOUCH

by Sheila Benson

From: *Los Angeles Times,* March 18, 1988.

1   "The Milagro Beanfield War," part magical fable, part realistic comedy-drama, is a
2 warmly intentioned, well-acted film full of a love of land and of people. You can tell that
3 from the way director Robert Redford lingers on a cobalt-blue New Mexico sky, or quick-
4 sketches the good, weathered faces of the villagers of Milagro itself.
5   Within the first few minutes, we've a hint of the picture's strengths and its shortcom-
6 ings. They come as much from David Ward and John Nichols's adaptation of Nichols's
7 own dense novel as from the hands of director Redford—also the film's co-producer, with
8 Moctesuma Esparza. For all its good liberalism, the movie's political and magical views
9 haven't progressed much further than Frank Capraville.
10   Redford has soaked the film in reverence—yet for all its realism, nothing feels real.
11 (That music for instance, that could have used a scratchy, lonesome Ry Cooder edge, is by
12 Dave Crusin, a different, far more mainstream sound.) For that matter, the writers' idea of
13 what's magic isn't very magical. And so it sits uneasily between the two styles.
14   In shaping a film with other-worldly elements which becomes a battle between simple
15 good and powerful evil, the story has to be grounded in something tough and believable.
16 Milagro is a depressed town, a dying one. We can see that. But it is touched throughout the
17 film by the Coyote Angel—the past, a vanished way of life—and these delicate <u>visitations</u>
18 remove the town's toughness and leave us only a cloying essence.
19   By the time the hardness enters Milagro with a very real shooting—more than two-
20 thirds of the way through the film's two hours—it's jarring and it's too late. The town has
21 an all-enveloping caul of sweetness. (The giant pink pig belonging to old Amarante is
22 certainly part of it, but on this point, all critical functions cease—that is one sensational
23 pig.)
24   The <u>hub</u> of the action occurs as Joe Mondragon (Chick Vennera), a young husband
25 and father, diverts water from a huge development corporation's supply down into his
26 own dusty land. First accidentally, then as an act of defiance, he decides to use the water to
27 grow beans in his dead father's field again. (The film suggests that Joe's father and the
28 Coyote Angel are one and the same.)
29   This act of rebellion from one of Milagro's too-little-employed men, who are clearly
30 not being hired in the development's white-bread work force, sends shock waves to every
31 kitchen, barber shop, street corner, and bar in Milagro, and even to Ruby's Body Shop and
32 Pipe Queen, Ruby Archuleta, proprietor (the fiery—and funny—Sonia Braga).

33 It's seen as sedition, as suicide, as dangerous, and, in some quarters—primarily
34 Ruby's—as high time. Charley Bloom (John Heard), lawyer and publisher of the tiny local
35 paper, takes the news <u>warily</u> as befits a very 'ex'-activist.

36 The opposition, headed by land developer Ladd-Devine (Richard Bradford) and his
37 enormous righthand man, Horsethief Shorty (James Gammon, exceptionally fine), beefs
38 up its strength with a state undercover police agent, Mr. Montana (Christopher Walken), a
39 nasty piece of work. And the plot lines are drawn, clear as the melodramas of old.

40 You can see the reasons why Redford was not absolutely wrong for this material.
41 Clearly, he has a feeling for this extraordinary country and his casting choices are
42 distinctive. In the pivotal role of Amarante Cardova, Redford introduces 74-year-old
43 Mexican cinema veteran Carlos Riquelme, a sort of Latino S.Z. (Cuddles) Sakall to U.S.
44 audiences who will, without doubt, take him to their hearts.

45 Ruben Blades—who has put on weight and a certain (misleading) air of gravity for the
46 role of the town's canny, peaceable sheriff—may reach an even larger audience than he
47 did at the center of "Crossover Dreams."

48 Another singer, Freddy Fender, can be found as the town's mayor, Sammy Cantu.
49 And Daniel Stern appears as a wonderfully out-of-place New York University ethnogra-
50 phy student, Herbie Platz, whose wordless scenes <u>charting</u> his growing friendship with
51 Amarante form some of the movie's nicest moments. All up and down the film, there are
52 faces and voices that make it plain how important the right casting was to the film makers.

53 But, for all his ease with actors, Redford hasn't been able to pull these good individual
54 performers into anything like an ensemble. A few, a miscast Melanie Griffith and, in
55 particular, Christopher Walken, seem to be acting in some other picture entirely—in
56 Walken's case a far more menacing one.

57 And for all the film's almost shocking visual beauty (from cameraman Robbie
58 Greenberg), an overall unity that combines the visual and the storytelling, is missing.

59 It's pixilated and it's pleasant, but it remains a must-see only if you are a nut for the
60 antics of magnificent pigs.

Reading for Full Comprehension

1. What does "the two styles" on line 13 refer to?

2. T/F   The author feels this movie is realistic.

3. T/F   The author suggests that the director is solely responsible for the
   problems with this movie.

4. How does the author feel about the effect of "magic realism" in this picture?

5. Which movie scene would the author agree shows discrimination toward
   Mexican-Americans?

6. What opinion does the author give of the movie in the first paragraph?

7. Which sentence in the third paragraph is the thesis sentence of the review?

8. In line 26 the author uses the term "act of defiance." What phrase in the
   next paragraph means the same thing?

9. This reviewer says many of the things that the first reviewer said. In line 1, she calls it a "magical fable." In line 4, she uses the verb "sketches" to describe Redford's work. In line 9, she compares the movie to the work of Frank Capra. Reread the two reviews and explain how the two reviewers compare/contrast on these three points.
   A. Which reviewer felt the movie was most successful as a fable?
   B. Which reviewer gives a more extensive comparison of Redford to an artist?
   C. Which reviewer has a higher opinion of Frank Capra's style?

10. In movie reviews, the authors usually comment on several different parts of the movie, including the actors, the visual effects, the story of the movie, and the music. As you reread this review, fill in the following chart.

OPINION	GOOD	BAD	NO OPINION	SPECIFIC COMMENTS
Cast in general				
actor 1 Ruben Blades	X			may reach an even larger audience than he did at the center of "Crossover Dreams"
actor 2				
actor 3				
actor 4				
actor 5				
actor 6				
actor 7				
Visual effects				
Story of the movie				
Music				

11. Summarize this reading selection in 75 to 100 words.

WRITING ASSIGNMENTS

1. Pretend you are Herbie Platz. Write a brief, one-to-two-page report for your sociology class, on the culture of the New Mexicans. In the introduction, identify the place and the people with whom you made your observations. In the body, record your observations. Limit your comments to two or three specific points, such as religion, family life, or political beliefs.

2. Pretend you are the mayor of Milagro. You think the Miracle Valley Recreation Area will help Milagro. Write a letter to the newspaper explaining why the recreation area is a good idea and encouraging the people of Milagro to support it.

3. Pretend you are Ruby Archuleta. You don't think the Miracle Valley Recreation Area will help Milagro. Write a letter to the newspaper explaining why the recreation area should not be permitted in Milagro.

4. Write a brief two-page history paper. In your paper, explain the history of New Mexico and the Spanish-American land wars.

5. Compare and contrast the opinions of the two reviewers about the movie. You may wish to write a paragraph about one review and then a second paragraph about the other review in which you compare/contrast it to the first review.

6. Compare and contrast the indigenous culture of the New Mexicans with the culture of the Amish, whom you learned about in the movie *Witness*. In what ways are the cultures similar? In what ways are they different? Limit your paper to an in-depth examination of two or three cultural points.

4

RACISM AND EDUCATION: A CASE STUDY

A. What subject is being taught in this classroom?

B. How is this classroom similar to/different from your high school?

INTRODUCTION

Vocabulary in Context

Directions: Read the following passage without using your dictionary. As you read the passage, try to guess the meaning of the following words, all of which are underlined in the passage. Write your guesses in the appropriate column and then look up the words in an English-English dictionary to check your guesses. After that, reread the passage, using your dictionary, and do the exercises at the end of the passage.

Words	My Guess	Dictionary Definition
affluent		
allocated		
acute		

1 The United States guarantees a free public education to all citizens. In theory, this is
2 supposed to provide equal opportunity for all to obtain a minimum level of education. In
3 practice, however, the opportunity to achieve such a level is not equal because public
4 school education in the United States is not standardized.
5 Public schools in the United States are governed by local school boards, which set
6 curricula and pay for education by using a percentage of local tax money. More affluent
7 areas, with more tax money to spend on education, have a definite advantage over poorer
8 areas, where little money can be allocated to education. Poor schools are also often located
9 in inner cities, where social problems such as drugs, crime, and juvenile delinquency are
10 more acute than in affluent areas.
11 The question now before the United States is how to equalize the level of education
12 for all. Various solutions to this problem have been suggested.
13 One solution of the past few decades has been the use of standardized examinations.
14 College entrance exams such as the SAT (Scholastic Aptitude Test) offer educators a way
15 of measuring equality of students from diverse backgrounds. Recently, however, such

16 exams have been questioned. If in fact students have unequal educational opportunities,
17 then how can tests like these measure equality?

Reading for Full Comprehension

1. What words in the third sentence contrast with the words "in theory" in the second sentence?

2. List two <u>major</u> differences between poor and affluent schools.

3. T/F The author believes all United States students achieve the same minimum level of education.

4. T/F School curricula are the same for students in both affluent and poor areas.

5. T/F Standardized exams have existed for at least twenty years.

6. T/F Standardized exams are a popular way of helping students achieve equality.

READING #1

Prereading

Directions: These are some words that you will need to understand before reading the passage.

at risk (adj.): a term applied to students who are in danger of not succeeding, usually because of a nonacademic reason.

Department of Education (proper noun): a federal government office that oversees public education in the United States.

Secretary of Education (proper noun): a federal cabinet member, the head of the Department of Education.

Superintendent of Education (proper noun): the head of each local school board in the United States. Each state also has a Superintendent of Education.

to make headlines (verbal idiom): to get a lot of attention and publicity.

Vocabulary in Context

Directions: Read the following passage without using your dictionary. As you read the passage, try to guess the meaning of the following words, all of which are underlined in the passage. Write your guesses in the appropriate column before looking up the words in an English-English dictionary to check your guesses. Then reread the passage, using your dictionary, and do the exercises at the end of the passage.

Words	My Guess	Dictionary Definition
spur		
lashed out		
rhetoric		
foundered		
localities		
incentives		

"Sequ" is a root that means "follow." What do you think a sequel to a report might be?

_____

A NEW BATTLE OVER SCHOOL REFORM
Criticism greets a tough report on progress in U.S. classrooms

by Lara Brown

1   Few government documents have raised more hackles or lit more fires than the 1983
2 Department of Education report titled "A Nation at Risk." The survey sounded an alarm
3 over the "rising tide of mediocrity" sweeping American schools. It warned that had this
4 mediocrity been imposed by a foreign power, "we might well have viewed it as an act of
5 war." Overnight, the document became a spur for nationwide school reform.
6   Last week at the White House on the fifth anniversary of "A Nation at Risk," Secretary
7 of Education William Bennett presented President Reagan with a sequel that is likely to be
8 even more controversial. Titled "American Education: Making It Work," the new report
9 tries to assess what the reform movement has achieved during the past half decade.
10 "There has been undeniable progress," proclaimed the Secretary. "Students have made
11 modest gains." But, he concluded, "we are still at risk."
12   On the positive side, Bennett pointed to a small increase (16 points out of 1,600) in
13 SAT scores, ending a long, downward slide; a jump from 76 percent to 86 percent in the
14 percentage of high school seniors passing American history; and new or strengthened
15 homework policies among at least one-fourth of all high schools. But the report's
16 downbeat observations quickly overshadowed those cheering facts. Items:

17   • *"Good schools for disadvantaged and minority children are*
18   *much too rare [and] the dropout rate among blacks and Hispanic*
19   *youth in many of our inner cities is perilously high."*
20   • *"Teachers and principals are too often hired and promoted in*
21   *ways that make excellence a matter of chance, not design."*
22   • *"Our schools still teach curricula of widely varying quality."*
23   • *"Students know too little and their command of essential skills*
24   *is too slight."*

25   Bennett lashed out at those who he believes are to blame: the "educational establish-
26 ment" and, particularly, teachers' unions. "You're standing in the doorways, you're
27 blocking up the halls of education reform," he charged. Bennett assailed those who
28 engage in what he calls "opposition by extortion, the false claim that to fix our schools will
29 first require a fortune in new funding." Instead, Bennett somewhat vaguely recommends

³⁰ strengthening curriculums, rewarding good teachers and principals, and instituting
³¹ "accountability" throughout the education system.
³²   The new report has angered many educators, who resent Bennett's emphasis on the
³³ negative, his slighting of the achievements of the past five years, and his finger pointing.
³⁴ "Sarcastic, belittling, patronizing," declared John Brademas, president of New York
³⁵ University and formerly a leading education advocate in Congress. California Superinten-
³⁶ dent of Public Instruction Bill Honig notes that the number of students scoring above 450
³⁷ in math and 500 in verbal on SATs has jumped 18 percent since 1983. "If this was the steel
³⁸ industry and we had an 18 percent gain in productivity, it would make headlines," says
³⁹ Honig. The downbeat report, he adds, "misleads the public."
⁴⁰   Yet even Bennett's critics agree that American schools need further improvement.
⁴¹ The past five years has indeed brought about tighter graduation requirements and stricter
⁴² teacher standards backed by better pay. But most of the progress has come in affluent
⁴³ areas where students are best equipped to respond to increased demands. "The reform
⁴⁴ movement has been most successful with those students who need it the least," says Ernest
⁴⁵ Boyer, president of the Carnegie Foundation for the Advancement of Teaching. For
⁴⁶ inner-city students there has been little change. "Reforms were aimed at middle-class
⁴⁷ schools," notes Gary Orfield, an urban education expert at the University of Chicago.
⁴⁸ "They didn't really address low-income schools."
⁴⁹   . . . Extra help for students, particularly in crumbling urban schools, requires
⁵⁰ extra money. While most states have raised their education budgets since 1983, the
⁵¹ Federal Government's contribution has been largely rhetoric. "I just wish that the policies
⁵² of the President and Secretary matched their verbal commitment," says Brademas.
⁵³ Bennett's talk of a conspiracy of "extortion," say his critics, closes the door to intelligent
⁵⁴ discussion of funding.
⁵⁵   So far, most of the thrust for reform has come from governors, legislators, and
⁵⁶ businessmen concerned about a shrinking pool of qualified workers. "Reform has been a
⁵⁷ sort of top-down initiative," says John Moore, chairman of the department of education at
⁵⁸ Trinity University in San Antonio. "Teachers were never brought into it." As a result,
⁵⁹ while progress was made, many reforms were misguided. In Houston, for instance, state
⁶⁰ rules requiring failing students to be tutored foundered because of problems in schedul-
⁶¹ ing the sessions and the fact that many students failed to show up.
⁶²   More than that, in part because of Bennett's broadsides, teachers were considered the
⁶³ problem, which left them wary of the reformers. "The constant criticism is demoralizing,"
⁶⁴ complains Albert Shanker, head of the American Federation of Teachers. "If the
⁶⁵ Secretary of Commerce disliked businessmen as much as Bennett dislikes teachers, the
⁶⁶ president would throw him out of the Cabinet."
⁶⁷   Ultimately, most educators agree, if reform is to have any lasting success, it will have to
⁶⁸ turn away from such externally imposed regulations and encourage change from within.
⁶⁹ Principals and teachers, says P. Michael Timpane, president of Teachers College at
⁷⁰ Columbia University, "have got to be at the center of reform." Some localities have already
⁷¹ realized this. In New Jersey, Commissioner of Education Saul Cooperman has sought to
⁷² create teacher incentives, including bonuses for success in inner-city schools and grants
⁷³ for top teachers to spend in classrooms as they wish. Last fall Rochester teachers signed an
⁷⁴ innovative three-year contract granting greater classroom freedom and salaries that start

75 at $29,000 and rise to $70,000 for stars. In return, the teachers agreed to be held
76 accountable for student performance.
77   . . . Efforts like these, says Boyer, constitute a "new agenda," a critical second wave
78 that may succeed where the earlier, top-down reform movement failed. If so, perhaps at
79 last the tidal wave of mediocrity will subside.

Reading for Full Comprehension

A common strategy in building convincing arguments is the use of comparisons in the conditional form. When the author is trying to make a point, he or she can draw a comparison to a similar situation involving different elements, and, therefore, create a different outcome. Such a strategy not only illustrates the point, but also strengthens it and makes it more valid.

1. Look at the conditional/comparison on lines 3, 4 and 5. The author compares the increase in mediocrity to foreign intervention. How should we view mediocrity according to this comparison?

2. In lines 37 and 38, education is compared to _____.
    SAT score gains are compared to _____.
    How should we view a gain in SAT scores according to this comparison?

3. In lines 64–66, the Secretary of Commerce is compared to _____
    _____; teachers are compared to _____.
    What should the President do to Bennett according to this comparison?

4. The author uses the words "rising tide" on line 3 and "tidal wave" on line 79. What is he comparing mediocrity to?

5. What did the survey mentioned in line 2 warn about?

6. Why is its sequel likely to be controversial?

7. List three positive changes mentioned in the report.

8. List five negative points made in the report.

9. Who is the author of the report?

10. In what year was the report written?

11. Whom does Bennett blame for the problems in United States schools?

12. What response to the report does Bennett probably expect?

13. The author uses the word "lashed out" on line 25. What other word in the same paragraph means the same thing?

14. List two recent improvements in United States schools mentioned in the sixth paragraph. Which schools have benefited most from these reforms?

15. What is given as the reason why reform has not always been well directed? What are some ways of changing the present system of top-down reform?

16. Look at the word "vaguely" in line 29 and the punctuation around the word "accountability" in line 31. What can you infer about the writer's attitude toward Bennett's recommendations?

17. T/F   Prior to 1983, SAT scores had been declining.

18. T/F   SAT scores have been improving less in California than in the nation as a whole.

19. T/F   American history graduates are one measure of a school's success.

20. T/F   Bennett agrees that education first needs additional funding.

21. Summarize this reading selection in 75 to 100 words.

READING #2

Prereading

Directions: These are some words that you will need to understand before reading the passage.

affirmative discrimination (noun phrase): a pun, play on words, on the term affirmative action. Affirmative action is a policy adopted by institutions and businesses in the United States. This policy requires employers to consider job applicants' race, sex, physical ability, and age, to ensure that they are not discriminated against because of their race, sex, disability, or age. Some opponents of this policy claim that it actually discriminates against people who are <u>not</u> members of protected minority groups.

reverse discrimination (noun phrase): discrimination against a person or group to avoid discrimination against another person or group.

Vocabulary in Context

Directions: Read the following passage without using your dictionary. As you read the passage, try to guess the meaning of the following words, all of which are underlined in the passage. Write your guesses in the appropriate column and then look up the words in an English-English dictionary to check your guesses. After this, reread the passage, using your dictionary, and do the exercises at the end of the passage.

Words	My Guess	Dictionary Definition
incongruity		
depiction		
postulates		
prevailing		

"Re" is a prefix that can mean "again." "Concep" is a root that means "idea" or "thought." What does it mean to reconceptualize something?

RACE AND RACISM

Excerpted from: "A Special Issue: Race, Racism, and American Education: Perspectives of Asian Americans, Blacks, Latinos, and Native Americans" *Harvard Educational Review,* 58, no. 3, pp. v–vii. Copyright © 1988 by the President of Harvard College. All rights reserved.

1   Race and racism are central themes in the origin and development of the political,
2 social, and economic structure of the United States. Indeed, in this nation, race and racism
3 are defining concepts—concepts that shape our understanding of ourselves and our
4 relationships to others. The defining function of race and racism is seldom acknowledged
5 in U.S. social mythology, which depicts the "founders" of this country as fugitives from
6 tyranny, struggling to secure a place where all can be treated equal; a place of the people,
7 by the people, and for the people. Such is the mythology. Reality differs. Indeed, it was the
8 "founders" who passed the Nationalization Law of 1790 that not only defined the norms
9 and conduct of potential citizens, but also depicted the race—White.[1]
10   The incongruity between America's social mythology and its reality is not limited to
11 the depiction of the past. It is present in our contemporary understanding of the social

[1] Ronald T. Takaki, *Iron Cages: Race and Culture in Nineteenth-Century America* (New York: Alfred A. Knopf, 1979), p. 5.

12 functioning of the United States. This country, in fact, has constructed a contemporary
13 social mythology that relegates race and racism to the morgue. According to this new
14 mythology, the death of racism makes race itself an outdated concept. Moreover, when
15 race-based considerations and policies are advocated, they are seen merely as self-serving
16 actions designed to give unfair advantage to people of color. It is within this new
17 mythology, which <u>postulates</u> the death of racism, that predictable concepts such as reverse
18 discrimination and affirmative discrimination have emerged.
19   The influence of the new mythology on education can be seen in the widespread
20 adoption of the notion of "at-risk," which serves to mask the concept of race. When
21 students are classified as "at-risk," they are considered to be in danger of not completing
22 school and thereby increasing their chances of being nonproductive members of society.
23 "At-risk" students are those who possess characteristics found among students who often
24 do not make it through the system: poor, minority, and non-English speaking, to name a
25 few. While it is true that students with these characteristics are "at-risk," the question is,
26 why? Clearly, the <u>prevailing</u> belief among educators is that whatever the causes are, they
27 emerge from the lives, abilities, skills, families, or communities of the "at-risk" students.
28   This way of conceptualizing the educational status of minority students implies that
29 the subjects cause their own conditions and is an illustration of how educators have
30 adopted the new mythology of the death of race and racism. For example, most educators
31 will speak of "the 42 percent dropout rate among Hispanic high school students," or "the
32 low math and science achievement rates among minority students." Yet seldom do we hear
33 these same educators speak of "the failure of schools to graduate 42 percent of all Latino
34 students," or "the ineffectiveness of common approaches to math and science education."
35 Language reflects thinking, and thinking defines what it is possible to achieve. We will
36 never change the condition of education of students of color if we do not <u>reconceptualize</u>
37 our visions of Asian American, Black, Latino, and Native American students and acknowl-
38 edge that racism often prevails in our schools and institutions of higher learning.

Reading for Full Comprehension

1. T/F The idea most Americans have about the founders of this country is
   the correct one.

2. T/F Part of the belief most Americans have about their founders is that
   they were not racist.

3. T/F American citizenship laws have discriminated against nonwhite
   immigrants.

4. T/F Most Americans today have an accurate idea about race and racism.

5. T/F Most Americans would agree that race and racism are dead.

6. T/F Most Americans understand the need for policies such as Affirmative
   Action.

7. List the characteristics of at-risk students.

8. What do educators see as the reasons for "at-risk" students?

9. Why does the author reword the sentences on line 31, on lines 33–34?

10. T/F   The author would probably agree that a high dropout rate among Hispanic students is caused by racism.

11. Summarize this reading selection in 75 to 100 words.

READING #3

Vocabulary in Context

Directions: Read the following passage without using your dictionary. As you read the passage, try to guess the meaning of the following words, all of which are underlined in the passage. Write your guesses in the appropriate column and then look up the words in an English-English dictionary to check your guesses. Following this, reread the passage, using your dictionary, and do the exercises at the end of the passage.

Words	My Guess	Dictionary Definition
counterparts		
attributed to		
reconstructed		
eventuality		
reverberates		
deleterious		

STANDARDIZED TESTING AND MINORITY STUDENTS

by Robert L. Green and Robert J. Griffore

From: "Standardized Testing and Minority Students," The Journal of Negro Education, 49, no. 3, pp. 238–252.

1   Testing is pervasive and powerful in its influence on modern life. The negative
2 aspects of testing procedures are especially apparent with respect to racial minorities,
3 since tests can serve as a convenient tool for rationalizing discriminatory practices.
4 Because of past discrimination in all aspects of American life, racial minorities as a group
5 have not performed well on standardized tests when compared with their white counter-
6 parts. To the extent that this difference has been attributed to genetic factors, some
7 educators might have reached the conclusion that minorities cannot be expected to
8 perform acceptably in educational or employment settings. When, however, the experi-
9 ences of one group of test subjects have been marked by inferior schools, inferior housing,
10 inferior opportunities for employment, inferior incomes, and inferior health care, it is
11 difficult to imagine that their innate abilities would allow them to compete on an equal
12 basis with members of a group not similarly and deliberately discriminated against. It is
13 imperative to reserve judgment concerning innate abilities until society had been recon-
14 structed to provide equality from the very beginning in all areas of life for all citizens.
15   In addition to issues related to the general discrimination in American life, a
16 consideration of current testing practices requires attention to two specific issues: unfair-
17 ness in the tests themselves and unfairness in the use of tests and test scores.
18   Unfairness in the test itself, or test bias, is present when a test does not measure the
19 same dimensions of achievement across different groups. Test bias can, first, be due to the
20 content of the test. Test constructors have traditionally been white and middle class. In
21 addition, "tryout groups" for standardized tests may fail to include minority children, with
22 the result that too many questions inappropriate for such children are included. Dialect or
23 language differences between majority and minority students also can be a source of bias.
24 And certain test items may have irrelevant difficulty for children of low socioeconomic
25 status (by calling for middle-class common knowledge, for example).
26   Test bias can also arise from inappropriate test norms. The issue is the selection of the
27 samples of students used in establishing a "national norm." If the sample leaves out or
28 misrepresents some major ethnic, racial, regional, community-type, or income group, the
29 term "national norm" is a misrepresentation. There may be occasions when school systems
30 or researchers need to make group comparisons for evaluation purposes; however, it
31 should never be necessary to compare *individual* elementary school children to "national
32 norms."

33   Other problems emerge when scores are reported as grade equivalents, which may
34 easily be mistaken for standards of minimum performance. Teachers and principals want
35 all of their students to score at or above grade level. When some do not—an almost certain
36 eventuality—it is tempting to judge the low-achieving students as inherently inadequate.
37 If between-child comparisons need to be made, local norms are more appropriate.

38   Text validity can also be harmed by "atmosphere variables"—such things as speeded-
39 ness (time allowed for testing), testwiseness, answer-sheet format, item type, examiner
40 characteristics, expected use of the test results, and achievement motivation. . . .

41   Other factors may influence test performance—test anxiety, for example. To the
42 extent that anxiety acts as a debilitating factor, test performance is motivated by fear of
43 failure, which might result in lower test performance. Indeed, performance on the SAT
44 has been found very susceptible to examinees' anxiety. And test anxiety appears to be
45 inversely related to social class and also more prevalent among minority examinees.
46 Different cognitive styles and students' academic self-concepts are likely to influence
47 aptitude test scores as well. . . .

48   Test bias and the misuse of tests can have a negative impact which reverberates
49 throughout society. That a particularly deleterious effect is felt by minorities has been
50 emphasized by the literature. Yet the testing companies continue to prosper. For the
51 protection of future generations, it is time to check the unmonitored and uncontrolled
52 growth of the testing industry.

Reading for Full Comprehension

1. How can test scores be used against members of a minority?

2. The author presents two opinions why minority students do not do well on tests. What are those two opinions? Which one does the author believe is the correct reason? Does he believe that the other opinion should not be believed at all?

3. What is another word in paragraph one that refers to the same idea as "genetic factors?"

4. Which two testing issues does the author concentrate on?

5. How does the author define "test bias"?

6. In the third paragraph the author lists four examples to explain his topic sentence. Underline the topic sentence and list the four examples.

7. The author discusses two types of comparisons that are made with tests. Which type does the author believe may be needed? Which type does he oppose?

8. List the different atmosphere variables that can influence test validity.

9. List the three reasons for poor test scores given in the second to the last paragraph.

10. If the writer were to add one more paragraph, what kind of information/ opinions do you think it might contain? Explain your answer.

11. Summarize this reading selection in 75 to 100 words.

```
┌─────────────────────────────┐
│                             │
│     READING #4              │
│                             │
└─────────────────────────────┘
```

Prereading

Directions: These are some words that you will need to understand before reading the passage.

Bar Association (compound noun): an association of lawyers.

consumer watchdog (compound noun): consumer protection specialist.

red-faced (adj.): embarrassed.

to hold one's own (verbal idiom): to be competitive with.

to touch a raw nerve (verbal idiom): to bother or disturb.

Vocabulary in Context

Directions: Read the following passage without using your dictionary. As you read the passage, try to guess the meaning of the following words, all of which are underlined in the passage. Write your guesses in the appropriate column and look up the words in an English-English dictionary to check your guesses. Then reread the passage, using your dictionary, and do the exercises at the end of the passage.

Words	My Guess	Dictionary Definition
dispute		
defective		

Words	My Guess	Dictionary Definition
slights		
gist		
concedes		
forfeit		
maligned		
impair		

"Pre" is an affix meaning "before." "Dict" is a root meaning "say." What does it mean to say a test is a predictor of academic success?

SCORING CONTROVERSY TESTS LATINO COMMUNITY PRIDE

by Frank del Olmo

From: Los Angeles Times, Dec. 16, 1982.

1 The Educational Testing Service is probably so accustomed to national controversy by
2 now that the current dispute involving Garfield High School students must seem like a
3 minor irritant. But its officials should not underestimate the depth of feeling in Los
4 Angeles's Chicano community over the way events unfolded.

5   The testing service, a nonprofit corporation based in Princeton, N.J., administers
6 standardized tests for everyone from high-school juniors to applicants for law school and
7 other professional and graduate programs. Two years ago, no less a consumer watchdog
8 than Ralph Nader charged that the service's college admission tests were biased in favor of
9 students from upper income families and had little value as a <u>predictor</u> of future
10 performance.
11   Last year, service officials were red-faced when <u>defective</u> questions were found in
12 four different tests—including the all-important Scholastic Aptitude Test which helps
13 determine where thousands of high-school students will attend college.
14   Given this context, it's easy to see why the service might not pay much attention to the
15 protests of the Mexican-American Bar Association, the Mexican-American Education
16 Commission and other groups over the treatment of fourteen youngsters from East Los
17 Angeles. But the service's actions have touched a raw nerve in a community that is
18 understandably sensitive about unwarranted <u>slights</u> against its young people.
19   The <u>gist</u> of the Garfield High incident is this:
20   Last May, 18 students took an advanced calculus placement test administered by the
21 testing service. All passed—seven with a perfect score of 5 points, four others with 4
22 points. A few weeks later, according to Jaime Escalante, their mathematics teacher,
23 fourteen of the students received letters from the testing service asking questions about
24 their performance. The service wanted to know why the students solved a particular
25 problem in exactly the same way, and why they had similar answers on the multiple-choice
26 portion of the examination.
27   Escalante, a demanding instructor, who insists that his advanced math students work
28 after school hours and use college level textbooks, said that the explanation can be found
29 in his highly structured teaching methods. He emphasizes a step-by-step approach to
30 problem solving and a methodical answering process that often involves graphs.
31   While he <u>concedes</u> that the technique might seem rigid, it has proved remarkably
32 successful in preparing Garfield students to take advanced math classes. Escalante began
33 using his method at Garfield in 1979, and each year since the number of students taking
34 trigonometry and calculus classes has increased. At the same time, the number who passed
35 the testing service's standardized tests increased from four in 1979 to eight in 1980 to a
36 high of fifteen in 1981.
37   That explanation was not good enough for the testing service. It insisted that the
38 students either <u>forfeit</u> their high scores or take the test again. Twelve chose the latter
39 option (the other two had already left school). On the retest, all twelve passed again—with
40 five scoring 5 points and four scoring 4. All but one of the students have graduated and are
41 attending such colleges as Columbia, Princeton, UC Berkeley, USC, and UCLA.
42   Not surprisingly, many numbers of the school staff suspect that these students were
43 subjected to such a forceful challenge because they were Latinos attending an inner-city
44 school.
45   Spokesmen for the testing service deny that the incident had anything to do with the
46 students' ethnic background. They offer incredible explanations as to why test scorers
47 might have noted the similarity in answers and passed on a query to the testing service's
48 review boards, which handle all dealings with individual students.
49   But if the testing service's caution is understandable, so is the anger at Garfield.
50 Teachers and parents are so used to hearing about problems at Eastside schools—such as

51 gangs, graffiti, and dropout rates—that when there is a cause for genuine pride it is doubly
52 frustrating to have its validity questioned. Here were fourteen smart Latinos doing extra
53 work in a difficult subject and holding their own with the best young minds in the country.
54 And how does it get into the news? When some faraway testing agency suggests that
55 somebody may be cheating.
56   As if that were not enough, the testing service has also refused to discuss the Garfield
57 case with anyone but the students and their families on privacy grounds. So far, the service
58 has ignored requests for explanations and apologies from Escalante, other Garfield
59 teachers and counselors, and the principal, Henry Gradillas.
60   Gradillas wants the students' original test scores reinstated and not just as a matter of
61 principle. By scoring well some of the former Garfield students received college credit for
62 the advanced work that they did in high school. Those who didn't score as well the second
63 time may have to take a freshman math course that they could have avoided. Also, he
64 wants an apology, because he believes that Garfield's reputation has been unfairly maligned.
65 <u>maligned.</u>
66   Escalante also wants the original scores reinstated, although it was he who finally
67 urged his students to retake the calculus test lest further delays affect their chances of
68 attending the colleges of their choice. He is uncomfortable with all the publicity, and
69 worries that the continuing controversy may begin to <u>impair</u> his teaching.
70   That seems unlikely. He teaches a hard subject and is very demanding of his students,
71 but his enthusiasm for his work is obvious. And, as many other math teachers were
72 succumbing to the lure of private industry, Escalante gave up a position with a major
73 engineering company, to return to teaching, his field in his native Bolivia.
74   One can't help but admire Escalante's energy in the classroom as he rapidly writes
75 equations on the blackboard prodding his students while he addresses them with playful
76 nicknames like "Secret Agent" and "Marching Band." He is clearly one of those special
77 teachers who deserve far more support and encouragement than they get. It's too bad that
78 when recognition came he wasn't allowed to enjoy it.

Reading for Full Comprehension

1. How many different controversies involving tests has the Educational
    Testing Service been involved in in the last two years?

2. What did Ralph Nader accuse the tests of?

3. Why were the students from Garfield High School asked questions about
    their placement test?

4. List some of the people and groups that supported the students in the
    controversy.

5. Give two different opinions about the influence of the students' ethnic
    background on the controversy.

6. What do Gradillas and Escalante want the Educational Testing Service to
    do about the controversy over scores? Why?

7. Why has the number of students who pass the calculus placement test readily increased?

8. According to the author, will this controversy hurt Escalante's teaching? Why or why not?

9. Why does the author ask and then answer a question on lines 54 and 55?

10. Summarize this reading selection in 75 to 100 words.

THE MOVIE: STAND AND DELIVER

Photofest

A. What is the man doing?

B. What ethnic group are these people from?

About the Movie

Directions: Divide the following passage into phrases; locate primary word-group stress; then locate the primary sentence stress. Following the instructions at the end of the passage, locate emphatic stress. Practice reading the passage aloud and discuss it with a classmate.

The movie, *Stand and Deliver,* is set in a run-down, poor, neglected neighborhood of an East Los Angeles barrio, a neighborhood of people of Hispanic background. It is Jaime Escalante's first day at work as a Math/Computer Science teacher at Garfield High School, a local school.

As he enters the main office on his first day, he overhears conversations about the various disasters and emergencies that happened that day. He is also informed by the head of the mathematics department that there are no computers and she does not expect them to arrive. He will be teaching mathematics.

He then meets his students, who are disrespectful, undisciplined, suspicious, hostile and, above all, not interested in studying math. Some do not have seats; some do not speak English. Escalante takes charge of the class from the first day. He establishes order and motivates his students to work and excel.

Movie Vocabulary

Directions: Study these words before watching the movie.

accreditation: legal permission given to a school to offer courses and degrees.

AP exam: an abbreviation for the Advanced Placement exam.

ganas: the Spanish word for "desire."

Hispanic surnames: last names that are common among Hispanic people.

innocent until proven guilty: the most basic idea of the American legal system, that an accused person is innocent until he/she is proven to be guilty.

orale: the Chicano Spanish word for "listen."

vatos: the Chicano Spanish word for "tough guy."

As You Watch the Movie

Directions: Read the following questions. Keep them in mind while you watch the movie. After the movie, discuss your answers to these questions with a small group of your classmates.

The movie tells the story of a high school math teacher who helps his math students to be successful not only in math, but also in their lives. Through his persistence and determination he teaches the students that with discipline and hard work they can achieve anything they want to.

What problems does Escalante face in his job? How does he overcome them? What problems do students face? How do they overcome them? How does Escalante get along with his colleagues? How do his students have to change their lives in order to study math? How does Escalante motivate his students? What are the parents' attitudes toward their childrens' efforts? What are some of the problems/opinions of the other teachers in the movie?

Postmovie Discussion Questions

1. What problems did you notice in the neighborhood, school, and classroom at the beginning of the movie?

2. How does Escalante react to the situation?

3. How do the students react to him?

4. What are some of the methods he uses to motivate the students?

5. What are some differences between Garfield High School and your high school?

6. Consider the scene in which all the teachers meet to discuss accreditation. What are some of the opinions/problems of the other teachers in the school?

7. What does Escalante teach students about life? How does he accomplish it?

8. How do Escalante's colleagues view him?

9. What problems do they foresee for Escalante and his students?

10. How does Escalante plan to solve these problems?

11. Who is Escalante's strongest opponent? Why?

12. How would you describe Escalante?

MOVIE REVIEW #1

Prereading

Directions: These are some of the words that you will need to understand before reading the passage.

E. F. Hutton commercial (noun phrase): a TV commercial in which a group of people listen very carefully to another person.

muckamucks (noun): important people.

school of hard knocks (noun phrase): the education one receives from having a series of difficult experiences.

sturm und drang (noun): from the German for "storm and stress."

[to] hang on someone's every word (verbal idiom): to listen very attentively.

Warner Bros. (proper noun): a movie production/distribution company.

Vocabulary in Context

Directions: Read the following passage without using your dictionary. As you read the passage, try to guess the meaning of the following words, all of which are underlined in the passage. Write your guesses in the appropriate column and look up the words in an English-English dictionary to check your guesses. Then reread the passage, using your dictionary, and do the exercises at the end of the passage.

Words	My Guess	Dictionary Definition
delusions		
junctures		
replicate		
launched		

A REVIEW OF *STAND AND DELIVER*

by James Lardner

From: "Films," The Nation magazine. The Nation Co., Inc. 1988.

1 I suppose it was unrealistic of me to think I would be able to say, after watching a
2 movie about the teaching of calculus, what calculus is; and I don't rightly know why I
3 expected the movie to convey some understanding of the techniques with which its real-

4 life hero, Jaime Escalante, manages to plant higher math in the heads of a fairly
5 ragamuffin bunch of Hispanic teenagers in East Los Angeles. Perhaps these delusions had
6 their roots in a recent article in the *New York Times,* which told of the long hours that Tom
7 Musca and Ramon Menendez, who collaborated on the screenplay, spent observing
8 Escalante at work; of the rocky journey that their project traveled en route to finding a
9 home with the public-television series "American Playhouse"; and of the astonished
10 reactions that the finished film, "Stand and Deliver," elicited from assorted Hollywood
11 muckamucks including the ones at Warner Bros. who eventually decided to let it into the
12 nation's movie theaters. "It puts Hollywood to shame," Jeffrey Katzenberg, chair of
13 Disney Studios, is reported to have said. (He added that since he didn't think Disney could
14 do the film justice, he wasn't interested in distributing it.)
15   When one does not live in Hollywood, one sometimes forgets how very little in the way
16 of unconventionality it takes to set the antennae of that tranquil community's leaders
17 aflutter. In this case, what seems to have done the job is the mere notion of using poor
18 people and slums as something other than a battleground between cops and drug
19 peddlers—that, and a middle-aged hero with more than the usual amount of waist and less
20 than the usual amount of hair. In form, "Stand and Deliver" sticks to familiar pathways.
21 Musca and Menendez may be young, but somebody—if not at UCLA, then over at the
22 school of hard knocks—has taught them the essential lesson of the new Hollywood: when a
23 story seems to be verging near some difficult intellectual or emotional question, you
24 DISSOLVE QUICKLY TO: ELSEWHERE. As a result, the audience of "Stand and
25 Deliver" is spared the trauma not only of watching Escalante's students come to terms with
26 calculus but of watching their transformation from hooligans and daydreamers into a
27 worshipful cadre that hangs on his every word like the extras in an E. F. Hutton
28 commercial. These things just happen, and mostly offscreen. It's too bad that footnotes
29 haven't become part of movie grammar; if they had, "Stand and Deliver" could instruct us,
30 at such troublesome junctures, to refer to the equivalent scenes in "Blackboard Jungle"
31 and "To Sir, With Love."
32   No doubt, if we could see the first draft of Musca and Menendez's screenplay, or
33 perhaps even the rough-cut of the film, we would learn more about life in Jaime
34 Escalante's classroom than we do from the 103-minute film on which Warner Bros. and its
35 market analysis people have conferred their approval. No doubt, too, we would know
36 something about how Escalante came to be the man he is, and what might happen if other
37 teachers tried to replicate his achievements. The film leaps over, or circles around, a host
38 of questions, and when the time comes for a climax, it homes in on a confrontation with the
39 Educational Testing Service—an enemy that, however deserving of our contempt, is
40 peripheral to the story. The ETS suspects Escalante's students of cheating. After some
41 Sturm und Drang involving a pair of ETS investigators . . . the class takes the test again,
42 and again performs splendidly. We never fully understand the "unusual agreement of
43 incorrect answers" that launched the investigation in the first place.
44   Like so many American movies of late, "Stand and Deliver" winds up being about grit
45 and determination and victory. It aims to leave us feeling all warm inside, albeit unbur-
46 dened by any fresh knowledge or insight, lest, in quest of these objectives, it commit the
47 high crime of taxing some part of the audience's patience. It should really have been called
48 "Stand Up and Cheer," and I suppose there are worse things to cheer than a film that
49 treats such an estimable man with such respect. Musca and Menendez have obviously

50 worked at capturing Escalante's patter, which is delightful. ("You burros have math in
51 your blood!" he tells his students. "Did you know that neither the Greeks nor the Romans
52 could deal with zero? It was your ancestors the Mayans who understood the concept of
53 zero.") [Edward James] Olmos, given a year to prepare for the role, studied Escalante
54 relentlessly, in person and on tape, put on forty pounds and had his hair plucked. The film
55 is well shot and nicely edited, and it has an altogether likable cast. What it lacks is the
56 quality that would truly have put Hollywood to shame: the sort of trust in its audience that
57 Escalante has in his.

Reading for Full Comprehension

1.   In the first paragraph the author states that he had two expectations when
     he went to the movie. What were they? Why did he have those expecta-
     tions?

2.   Summarize the main point of the *New York Times* article mentioned in the
     first paragraph in one sentence.

3.   By using the words "antennae" and "aflutter" on lines 16 and 17, the
     author compares Hollywood to _____.

4.   T/F   In the opinion of the reviewer, Hollywood is a fairly conventional
           community.

5.   What does "done the job," on line 17, refer to?

6.   According to the author, how does Hollywood *usually* portray poor people
     and slums?

7.   According to the author (in paragraph 2), what happens in the movie when
     a scene becomes interesting?

8.   According to the author, what information (scenes) is missing from the
     movie?

9.   What do you suppose the movies *Blackboard Jungle* and *To Sir, With Love*
     were about?

10. The author uses the words "footnotes," "grammar," and "first draft" in the
     second and third paragraphs. What is he comparing movies to?

11. T/F   The author implies that the original version of the movie is the same
           as the one which we have seen.

12. Fill in this chart with the reviewer's opinions of the parts of the movie.

	GOOD	BAD	SPECIFIC COMMENTS
Important questions raised by the movie			
The unity of the story of the movie			
The writers of the movie			
The dialog of the movie			
The main actor in the movie			
The cinematography/editing			
The cast			

13. Reread the sentence, "It aims . . . from line 45 to line 47. "Lest" means "so that (negative)." It is followed by verbs in the simple form.

   Example: "He studies hard lest he flunk" means "He studies hard so that he doesn't flunk."

   Now answer the following questions from this sentence:
   A. What reactions does this movie try to create in the audience?
   B. What does "these objectives" refer to?
   C. What does "it" on line 46 refer to?
   D. Why doesn't the movie try to give the audience new information?

14. Summarize this reading selection in 75 to 100 words.

MOVIE REVIEW #2

Prereading

Directions: These are some of the words that you will need to understand before reading the passage.

to be in the works (verbal idiom): to be planned.

to do a Robert DeNiro (verbal idiom): to prepare oneself physically for an acting job.

Vocabulary in Context

Directions: **Read the following passage without using your dictionary. As you read the passage, try to guess the meaning of the following words, all of which are underlined in the passage. Write your guesses in the appropriate column and then look up the words in an English-English dictionary to check your guesses. Then reread the passage, using your dictionary, and do the exercises at the end of the passage.**

Words	My Guess	Dictionary Definition
succumb		
inertias		
capacity		
obsessed		
luxuriant		
strands		
recurs		
compelling		

TO SEÑOR, WITH LOVE, BRAINS, AND GANAS
Triumph in the barrio

by Jack Kroll with Jennifer Foote in Los Angeles

1   After the surprising box-office success of "La Bamba" ($54 million to date), the
2 appearance of more films with Hispanic themes was inevitable. But *Stand and Deliver* is no
3 quickie follow-up. It has been in the works since 1983, when director Ramon Menendez
4 read a story in the *Los Angeles Times* about Jaime Escalante, a math teacher who had
5 worked wonders in an East Los Angeles barrio high school. After years of research,
6 writing, and the usual studio turndowns, the resulting movie turns out to be a terrific piece
7 of work, more exciting than "La Bamba." An exciting movie about a math teacher? Well,
8 "Stand and Deliver" is about the profound excitement of learning, of kids changing their
9 lives, meeting the challenge of a man who refuses to allow them to <u>succumb</u> to the <u>inertias</u>
10 of system and stereotype.
11   When Escalante (Edward James Olmos) arrives at Garfield High to teach computer
12 science, he finds no computers. What he does find is a blackboard jungle of overcrowded
13 classrooms, drugs, vandalism, and gym teachers teaching math. In fact, Garfield is about
14 to lose its accreditation. Taking over a math class, Escalante has to deal with attitudes like
15 "I don't need math, I got a solar calculator with my doughnuts."
16   The intrepid Escalante speaks the kids' languages—not only Spanish but street jive.
17 He's a dumpy, balding, bespectacled guy who can out-ace the street gangs, mock the kids'
18 machismo ("Is it true that intelligent people make better lovers?") while appealing to their
19 cultural pride (describing the mathematical genius of the ancient Mayas he says, "You
20 **burros** have math in your blood.") Eventually the burros become thoroughbreds driven by
21 their teacher, who reaches beyond the classroom into their lives. Setting up the school's
22 first class in calculus (to the consternation of the school administrators who think he's
23 pushing the kids beyond their <u>capacity</u>), Escalante has them take the difficult advanced-
24 placement test for college credit. They all pass, but their marks are challenged by the
25 testing service, which can't believe the scores. The ensuing climax is as gripping as any
26 thriller, and a hundred times more meaningful.
27   At a time when wrangling politicos, moral cretins, and drug-dealing dictators hog the
28 headlines, Jaime Escalante is an authentic American hero. Olmos gives a wonderful
29 performance, making the teacher not a plaster saint but a man so <u>obsessed</u> with his mission
30 that he can drive himself into being unfair (and into a heart attack). The 41-year-old
31 Olmos, who's best known for his Emmy-award winning role as the steely, brooding

32 Lieutenant Castillo on "Miami Vice" is a native of the East L.A. barrio where the story takes
33 place. The actor did a Robert DeNiro for his portrayal of Escalante, gaining 40 pounds
34 and having his <u>luxuriant</u> hair cosmetically thinned to a few forlorn <u>strands.</u> He also
35 observed Escalante for a month of the teacher's eighteen-hour days. "I didn't think he'd be
36 able to do me," says Escalante. "I have so many secret moves, I didn't think he'd get them."
37   The Bolivian-born Escalante, now 57, has become a legend at Garfield High. Only 2
38 percent of American high-school students even attempt the difficult AP calculus test, but
39 each year more and more Escalante-taught students take it—and pass. Last year 87
40 passed; this year 160 students will take the test. His method is summed up by two
41 photographs on his classroom wall, of basketball players shooting from outside and
42 inside—two perfect parabolas. "The students are drawn in," says Escalante, "because
43 there's an application to math they can relate to. The only thing the kids need to bring to
44 their class is *ganas.*" It's a word that <u>recurs</u> throughout the film and it means desire.
45 Escalante has generated so much ganas that the once-scorned Garfield has become a
46 mecca for barrio kids. And along with the inevitable gang jackets, more and more jackets
47 are seen bearing the words GARFIELD HIGH—AP CALCULUS.
48   **Gang fights:** Everyone connected with the movie had ganas, including the young
49 actors who play the students with great charm and quiet, forceful realism. The only one
50 with a reputation is Lou Diamond Phillips, who played rock star Ritchie Valens in "La
51 Bamba." Most of the others answered audition calls, such as Vanessa Marquez, who had to
52 take a three-hour bus trip both ways from her job at a fast-food restaurant. Cuban-born
53 writer-director Ramon Menendez, 38, spent two years writing the script with producer
54 Tom Musca. His idea was to make a film with none of the expected clichés—no phony
55 Latino emotional flare-ups, no bloody gang fights on the eve of the test. "Maybe the world
56 at large will see the film and realize something about the Latino experience, and see these
57 people as human beings just like them. It is a bridging movie, a healing movie." And, he
58 might have added, a tremendously <u>compelling</u> one.

Reading for Full Comprehension

1. What do *La Bamba* and *Stand and Deliver* have in common?

2. Why is the film exciting according to the reviewer?

3. How does Olmos portray the "hero"?

4. What is Escalante's opinion about Olmos's performance?

5. Why does the author talk about the gang jackets?

6. What does the author say about the other actors in the film?

7. What did Menendez try to accomplish in the movie?

8. Why is it "a bridging and healing" movie?

9. Why does the author write, "An exciting movie about a math teacher"?

10. If you were reading this for a review of the movie, what paragraphs could
    you skip reading?

11. What are some of the clichés that exist about the types of students portrayed in the movie?

12. Summarize this reading selection in 75 to 100 words.

WRITING ASSIGNMENTS

1. Write an essay in which you summarize different ways racism influences education. Start with a paragraph defining racism. Explain how and why the concept has changed over the years. Then, illustrate how new racism surfaces in education.

2. Take just one of the students. How does he/she change because of Escalante's class? Write a paragraph in which you describe the student and his/her life when he/she became Escalante's student. Why did he/she decide to change? How did he/she change inside and outside the class?

3. Compare and contrast a teacher you liked who has influenced your life with the way Escalante influenced his students' lives. Start with a description of Escalante, his teaching style, and his influence on his students. Then, describe your teacher, his/her teaching style and the influence he/she had on his/her students. Compare and contrast the two teachers, their methods of teaching and influence on their students' lives.

4. Pretend you are an administrator of an inner-city school. Your school is about to lose its accreditation. Write a report outlining solutions to these problems.

5. Compare and contrast the students in your high school and Garfield High School.

6. Is there discrimination in education in your country? Who is discriminated against? Why? What should be done about it? Write a paper describing the problem and giving possible solutions.

7. Interview a minority person who felt he/she was discriminated against in education. Why? In what way? What has she/he done about it? Write a report on your interview to share with your classmates.

8. What are your ideas about standardized testing? Explain your own experiences with standardized exams in a brief paper.

9. Write a paper in which you compare/contrast testing practices in your country with those of the United States.

10. Write a letter to the editor who wrote the piece "Scoring Controversy Tests Latino Community Pride." Take a pro-Educational Testing Service position. Explain why the Educational Testing Service had the right to question the scores.

5

THE ASIAN AMERICANS: THE ROAD TO ACCEPTANCE

Eugene Gordon

A. What country is this woman from?

B. What do you think is the relationship between the woman and the child?

INTRODUCTION

Vocabulary in Context

Directions: Read the following passage without using your dictionary. As you read the passage, try to guess the meaning of the following words, all of which are underlined in the passage. Write your guesses in the appropriate column and look up the words in an English-English dictionary to check your guesses. Then reread the passage, using your dictionary, and do the exercises at the end of the passage.

Words	My Guess	Dictionary Definition
ancestors		
adapting		
retaining		
abandoning		
dilemma		
resolve		
wrestle		

"-istic" is a suffix that can mean "full of." "Plural" is a root that means "more than one." What do you think "pluralistic society" means?

---

1 As you learned in the chapter on *Witness,* America is a land of immigrants who
2 arrived, in some cases, a generation ago and, in other cases, five hundred years ago. Many
3 Americans identify themselves according to where their <u>ancestors</u> came from. It is
4 common to hear Americans describe themselves in such terms as Irish-Americans, Italian-
5 Americans, African-Americans, Chinese-Americans, Arab-Americans, or Mexican-
6 Americans.
7 When immigrants come to the United States they are faced with <u>adapting</u> to a new
8 society while at the same time <u>retaining</u> their cultural identity and traditions. The task of
9 fitting in while not <u>abandoning</u> identity is one that can become a <u>dilemma</u> for recent
10 immigrants. Cultural conflicts are not always <u>resolved</u> in the first generation. Often the
11 second and the third generation, the children and grandchildren of immigrants, still
12 <u>wrestle</u> with what it means to be an American while continuing to be a good child or
13 grandchild to one who does not necessarily share the values of the larger society.
14 During the last two decades, the United States has seen a sharp increase in the number
15 of Asian immigrants, a group that started coming to this country in the late 1700s. While
16 this recent increase has contributed to the <u>pluralistic</u> nature of American society and to a
17 redefinition of what it means to be American, it has also forced us to examine prejudices,
18 stereotypes, and fears that we, as a society, may have about these new and not-so-new
19 Americans. This chapter will allow you to examine both the personal and social concerns
20 many Asian Americans face.

Reading for Full Comprehension

1. How does the author define "the second and third generation"?

2. In paragraph two the word "dilemma" is used. What other words in paragraph two define the dilemma?

3. Whom does the author mean with the words "to one who does not necessarily share the values of the larger society" on line 13?

4. According to the author, are most problems in adapting to a new culture worked out in the first generation?

5. In what ways do you think that the new Asian immigrants may have changed the definition of American?

READING #1

Prereading

Directions: These are some of the words that you will need to understand before reading the passage.

a line of reasoning (noun phrase): the structure of an argument.

clout (noun): power; influence.

driven (adj.): one who is highly motivated, almost too motivated.

hard scrabbling (adj.): one who struggles hard for something.

Harlem (noun): a section of New York City in which many blacks live.

high profile (adj.): that which can easily be seen or that which is highly publicized.

Hmong (noun): a group of people from Laos.

Ivy-League campuses (noun phrase): universities such as Harvard, Columbia, Yale, and Princeton.

Ku Klux Klan (proper noun): a racist organization that promotes the superiority of the white race. Burning wooden crosses (cross burning) and the wearing of white robes are common tactics used by this organization to create fear in those it opposes.

pressed (adj.): in the state of being financially drained.

to bring to a head (verbal idiom): to bring a bad situation to its worst point.

to picket (verbal idiom): to demonstrate by holding protest signs and walking in front of or near the area, the place, or event which is the subject of protest.

to sledgehammer (verbal idiom): to hammer with a sledgehammer, a powerful hammer.

turn of the century (adj.): typical of the style popular around 1900.

upward mobility (noun phrase): the ability to move to a higher social class.

Vocabulary in Context

Directions: Read the following passage without using your dictionary. After you have read the passage without a dictionary, try to guess the meaning of the following words, all of which are underlined in the passage. Write your guesses in the appropriate column and then look up the words in an English-English dictionary to check your guesses. Finally, reread the passage, using your dictionary, and do the exercises at the end of the passage.

Words	My Guess	Dictionary Definition
pariahs		
disgruntlement		
pinnacle		
harassment		
arsonists		
feuds		
culminated		
prevailed		

Words	My Guess	Dictionary Definition
slurs		
fatal		
animosity		
friction		
denounce		
undertaking		
lagged		
ambivalent		
moguls		
verdict		
indict		
inflammatory		

Improving your context guessing is often a question of using both grammatical and contextual information to improve your chances of guessing correctly. For example, consider the word "moguls" on line 129. Read the sentence carefully. What do we know that moguls can do?

If they can do that, then moguls must be (pick one): people, places, things. What is another word in the same paragraph that means the same as "moguls"?

PREJUDICE AGAINST ASIANS: ANXIETY AND ACCEPTANCE

by Karl Zinsmeister

Reprinted with the permission of the American Enterprise Institute for Public Policy Research, Washington, D.C.

1   The history of bigotry in the United States is one of steady disappearance, and
2   attitudes toward Asian-Americans are no exception. Starting out as <u>pariahs</u> ("the feeling
3   against the Chinaman . . . is more bitter and intolerant than that against the Negro,"
4   wrote one turn-of-the-century observer), Asian Americans came to be accepted and
5   admired as a model minority. But the last few years have brought some disquieting new
6   pressures against them. Success has its costs in jealousy and <u>disgruntlement</u> among the less
7   accomplished. At the bottom of the socioeconomic ladder in America's ghettos and
8   working-class neighborhoods, as well as in pockets at the very <u>pinnacle</u> of governmental,
9   corporate, and intellectual life, a new animosity toward Asians can be detected.

10 **HOMEGROWN HATREDS**

11 Figures from the Justice Department show a 62 percent increase in anti-Asian
12 incidents from 1984 to 1985. In Los Angeles County, Asians were targets of an astounding
13 50 percent of the racial incidents in 1986 (versus 15 percent in 1985). In Boston, a city
14 where Asian Americans make up a small fraction of the population, 29 percent of racial
15 crimes recorded by police were committed against Asian Americans in the latest year,
16 compared to just 2 percent five years earlier. Given their low numbers, inner-city Asian
17 Americans have been exposed to relatively high rates of racial <u>harassment</u>.
18 On Christmas Eve 1986 in Revere, Massachusetts, <u>arsonists</u> burned down a house
19 sheltering twenty-eight Cambodian immigrants. The incident was one in a dramatic series
20 of anti-Asian attacks in Revere, a working-class suburb of Boston. Rock and brick
21 throwing at Southeast Asian immigrants are everyday occurrences in the town. A long
22 string of beatings, vandalism, and attacks on property, carried out mostly by white
23 teenagers, dates back several years. A neighbor of one Southeast Asian family complained
24 to a *Wall Street Journal* reporter, "Immigrants used to come from countries nearly as

25 civilized as the United States. These people come from jungle communities." His street, he
26 says, "looks like a refugee camp." A former Revere city councilor whispers that, "The
27 rumor, strictly a rumor, is that they eat dogs."

28   In the early 1980s, several high-profile, occasionally violent, <u>feuds</u> developed be-
29 tween Vietnamese fishermen and Hispanic and American-born fishermen in Texas,
30 Florida, and California. Established fishermen complained that the Vietnamese repre-
31 sented unfair competition because they worked day and night. "They don't go in for a
32 beer. They don't go in to watch football. That makes other people mad," explained the
33 director of the Vietnamese Fishermen Association in Oakland, California. Some whole-
34 sale buyers refused to deal with Vietnamese. In Florida, a state law was passed prohibiting
35 the large nets used by the Vietnamese. In Texas, the state legislature put a two-year
36 moratorium on new shrimp-boat licenses in Galveston Bay and attempted to halt shrimp-
37 ing operations at 2 P.M. daily.

38   In Texas, arguments <u>culminated</u> in the shooting death of one white fisherman, the
39 burning of several Vietnamese boats, and the firebombing of a Vietnamese home and a
40 packing factory that employed many refugees. About two-thirds of the refugees fled to
41 another town as a result. Texas shrimpers invited Ku Klux Klan agitators to take part in
42 the dispute to draw attention to their complaints. Vowing to drive the Vietnamese off the
43 Gulf Coast, the Klansmen burned crosses, rode on fishing boats in robes, and threatened
44 buyers who dealt with the Vietnamese. Eventually, however, the Vietnamese <u>prevailed</u>. By
45 the mid-1980s, they dominated local operations and had won general acceptance.

46   Not all anti-Asian incidents are directed at recent immigrants. One of the most
47 notorious cases of the last few years involved a fully assimilated college-educated Chinese
48 American named Vincent Chin. Indictments alleged that while both men were drinking
49 heavily at a Detroit bar, laid-off autoworker Ronald Ebens directed racial <u>slurs</u> at Chin
50 and, mistaking him for a Japanese American, blamed him "for the problems of the ailing
51 Detroit automobile industry." The argument ended in the <u>fatal</u> clubbing of Chin, and
52 Ebens's conviction on manslaughter charges.

53 **BLACK RESENTMENTS**

54   While there have been controversies and violence between white blue-collar workers
55 and Asian immigrants in several spots around the country, the broadest, deepest, and
56 most sustained source of anti-Asian <u>animosity</u> in the United States today—and the one
57 conflict most clearly getting worse, not better—involves <u>friction</u> between blacks and Asian-
58 American entrepreneurs in low-income center-city neighborhoods. Los Angeles, Phila-
59 delphia, Harlem, Atlanta, Chicago, Washington, Peoria, New Orleans, Baltimore, Provi-
60 dence, Seattle–Tacoma, and other cities have seen clashes between blacks and Asian
61 Americans. In September 1986, Sarah Carter, a black resident of Washington, D.C.'s
62 economically pressed and nearly all black Anacostia neighborhood, got into a quarrel with
63 the owner of a local Chinese-American carryout food shop, which resulted in threats of
64 violence. At that point, owner Cheung Hung Chan chased Ms. Carter from the establish-
65 ment with an unregistered handgun.

66   Chan was arrested for firearms violations and eventually sentenced to 100 hours of
67 community service. But his store was closed down for several months by picketing,
68 vandalism, and threats. The gun incident had sparked a much deeper resentment.
69 According to one eyewitness, Carter said that while the immediate cause of the argument

70 was dissatisfaction with a food order, "She wanted to see the store closed anyway because
71 Chinese [shouldn't] be owning all these stores in the community."
72   The Rev. Willie Wilson, leader of the subsequent months-long boycott, put the
73 argument directly: "The Asian community is the latest of a series of ethnic groups that
74 have come into our community, disrespected us, raped us economically, and moved out at
75 our expense." He urged blacks to "support our own," and called for the removal of
76 nonblack businesses from black residential areas. "Our community cannot afford to have
77 Asians dominate the economics of our neighborhood," he stated.
78   Several black leaders disavowed the protest and its anti-Asian sentiment. But the
79 black city legislator representing the district stated in an October television interview:
80 "The day of the Asian community occupying or getting the majority of business in a [black]
81 neighborhood is over. . . . We are not going to burn down our community. . . . We
82 are going to use our clout in city hall."
83   While it is seldom publicly acknowledged by either group, friction between Asian
84 immigrants and blacks is a big issue at the grassroots level in American inner cities today.
85 To ignore this is to risk an eventual serious blowup.
86   Nineteen eighty-five saw a series of confrontations between Korean businessmen and
87 blacks in Harlem, where Korean Americans own about a quarter of the shops on the main
88 strips. Los Angeles has had a number of tense encounters, and at one point the Los
89 Angeles chapter of the NAACP called for a "selective buying campaign" against Asian
90 businesses.
91   The issue had been brought to a head by a series of articles in Los Angeles's Afro-
92 American newspaper, *The Sentinel,* which condemned the Asian shopkeepers' takeover of
93 businesses in black areas. In response to the series, the executive director of the Los
94 Angeles Commission on Human Relations objected that the term " 'the black community'
95 was used to describe a geographical area in which it seemed to be suggested that non-black
96 businesses were unwanted, almost an enroachment on private property."
97   Predominantly black West Philadelphia has also produced some ugly rhetoric and
98 tension. The proposed opening of one new Asian-run store prompted local black radio
99 personality and civil rights activist Georgie Woods to <u>denounce</u> Korean merchants on his
100 radio show. "They don't look like us, and they don't live like us, and they don't act like us."
101 In Washington, D.C., ten-year-old Ho Cheung tells of taunts and beatings and the refusal
102 of his black classmates to use his real name, calling him "Chop Suey" or "Ching Chong" or
103 "Chinky" instead.
104   Some Asian–black disputes have sprung from competition over jobs, social services,
105 and housing. A large number center on the opening and operation of small businesses, an
106 <u>undertaking</u> at which Asians excel and at which blacks have <u>lagged</u>. Most fundamentally,
107 the resentment stems from the rapidity with which newly arrived Asian immigrants have
108 progressed from poverty to economic security and the implicit indictment that presents to
109 low-income black Americans. Asian-American upward mobility is sometimes overstated.
110 It often comes at considerable personal cost (loss of leisure and deferral of pleasures to
111 subsequent generations, for example). And it is hardly automatic: In 1980, 18 percent of
112 Chinese-American families who had immigrated in the previous decade were still poor, as
113 were 15 percent of Koreans and 35 percent of Vietnamese Americans. But the perception
114 of effortless success often causes tension between Asian Americans and their less pros-
115 perous neighbors.

116 **PREJUDICE AT THE PEAK**

117   If the cultural distrust at the base of America's social pyramid often grows out of
118 economic competition, the same is also true among elites. The last half decade has not
119 been an easy one for American labor-union chiefs, executives of manufacturing corpora-
120 tions, government trade negotiators, and the millions of other Americans who depend
121 upon the health of these organizations for their own prosperity. American labor leaders
122 are displeased by the downward pressure exerted on U.S. wages by Japanese, Taiwanese,
123 and Korean competition. Labor groups have been known to sponsor public sledgeham-
124 merings of imported Asian products, and they would like to reduce flows of low-wage
125 immigrants into this country as well.

126   The attitudes of American businessmen have been more <u>ambivalent</u>. On one hand,
127 they are fascinated with Asian economic success and are willing to study, even copy, Asian
128 methods. On the other hand, the heat of high-stakes competition has accustomed auto,
129 chip, and steel <u>moguls</u> to thinking of our Asian trading partners not as allies but as
130 enemies. Once established, perceptions like that can take on a life of their own. There have
131 been times in the past when Asian-origin Americans have had the deeds of their ancestors
132 visited upon them and been unfairly judged and held accountable for foreign behavior. In
133 a time of tension with our overseas Asian trading partners, there may be some risk of that
134 at present as well.

135   The competitive anxiety Americans increasingly feel toward Asia has found its way
136 into not only industrial but also literary and intellectual spheres. One of the last articles
137 written by the late Theodore White was a cover story for the *New York Times* Magazine
138 suggesting that recent Japanese economic successes could be thought of as reversing the
139 <u>verdict</u> of World War II. A series of "Japan As Number One"-style books have fanned the
140 image of superhuman—and threatening—Asian achievement. More recently, a March
141 1986 article by Gore Vidal in *The Nation* contained this passage:

142   For America to survive economically in the coming Sino-Japanese world, an alliance
143   with the Soviet Union is a necessity. After all, the white race is a minority race with
144   many well-deserved enemies, and if the two great superpowers of the Northern
145   Hemisphere don't band together, we are going to end up as farmers or, worse, mere
146   entertainment for the more than one billion grimly efficient Asiatics.

147 Vidal is understated as a statistician (there are actually three billion Asiatics) but otherwise
148 quite expansive. His argument that Asians are so different, and so menacing, that even the
149 yawning political, economic, and cultural canyon that divides the Soviet Union and the
150 United States ought to be surmountable in comparison shows how far this sort of argu-
151 ment has gone in recent years.

152   It is a perverted but relatively short step from this line of reasoning to one that would
153 also <u>indict</u> Asians in America. Unfastidious acolytes of Lee Iacocca, Gore Vidal, and
154 Michigan Congressman John Dingell ("little yellow people") might be tempted to apply
155 their rhetoric a little closer to home. The possibility that incessant <u>inflammatory</u> state-
156 ments from American elites might eventually have an incendiary influence on mass
157 opinion and attitudes toward persons of Asian origin cannot be discounted. For that
158 matter, even among the fastidious, it is possible that a drumbeat of "The Asians are
159 coming!" in public arguments and media reports could eventually condition an uncon-
160 scious negative response to things and people of Asian origin.

161 COLLEGE QUOTAS

162   Some Asian-American activist groups would claim that such a response has already
163 occurred on the nation's campuses. In the last decade, the attitudes of college admission
164 officers toward Asian-American applicants have undergone a dramatic shift. In the
165 mid-1970s, Asian Americans received quota and other preferences and were admitted to
166 colleges at higher than average rates. Today, at America's best universities, Asian
167 Americans are being admitted at a rate one-third lower than Caucasians, despite compara-
168 ble or higher academic qualifications.
169   Asian Americans are indeed now "overrepresented" on Ivy League campuses,
170 comprising around 8 percent of the freshman classes, compared to under 3 percent of the
171 U.S. college-age population. In this they hardly represent the extreme, however. Jews, for
172 instance, who also make up under 3 percent of U.S. youth, are 25 to 30 percent of the
173 typical Ivy League student body.
174   In explaining the recent relatively low acceptance rate of Asian Americans, admis-
175 sions officers have argued that many Asian-American students are too narrowly focused
176 (business, engineering, pre-med), that they are less socially conscious and active, that they
177 are "driven." In the face of a substantial rise in college applications from Asian Americans
178 (because of increased immigration and rising scholastic ambitions) university officials have
179 become fearful of being "swamped" by Asian-American students.

180 ANXIETY AND ACCEPTANCE

181   Asian Americans are our most recently arrived minority and, unlike some other
182 groups, new waves of unassimilated Asian immigrants continue to flow into the country.
183 The hard scrabbling of unfamiliar people at the bottom of the social ladder always inspires
184 resentments. Usually, however, these are fairly short-lived. When a group of Hmong
185 tribesmen moved into tight-knit and rarely disturbed McDowell County in North
186 Carolina a few years ago, for example, there was an initial outburst of distrust from the
187 county's mostly white residents. But before long, Hmong were well-integrated into local
188 churches, employed at the nearby pharmaceutical and glass factories, and warmly
189 accepted. That's the American pattern: a wave of anxiety, followed by a welcoming
190 embrace.
191   What is happening in inner-city neighborhoods today is less encouraging. It is more
192 intractable, simply because so much about America's inner-city ghettos is intractable and
193 depressing. But, critically, it is clear that the sometimes hostile reception facing Asian
194 inner-city immigrants has not defeated them in their determined climb up the economic
195 ladder. It is merely causing more human anguish and ill feeling than is necessary.
196   As for the sometimes reckless rhetoric at the top of American society, that primarily
197 reflects the uncertain and insecure feeling we as a nation are now experiencing in the face
198 of stiff and apparently permanent new foreign competition. It will wane if and as we
199 demonstrate our ability to cope with that external competition. If that proves to be beyond
200 our capabilities, intolerance will be but a minor part of our problems.

Reading for Full Comprehension

1. In line 57, Zinsmeister uses the word "friction"; in line 68, the word "sparked"; in line 85 the word "blowup"; in line 139, the word "fanned"; in line 155, the word "inflammatory"; and in line 156, the word "incendiary." Look up any of these words you are unfamiliar with. The author suggests a comparison between anti-Asian feelings and _____.

2. In line 7, Zinsmeister uses the word "bottom"; in line 8 the word "pinnacle"; in lines 183 and 195 the word "ladder"; in line 117 the word "pyramid." Look up any of these words you are unfamiliar with. The author suggests a comparison between American society and _____.

    By associating society with this metaphor, what is Zinsmeister implying about the way one ethnic group sees other ethnic groups?

3. Zinsmeister uses in line 179 the word "swamped"; and in line 182, the word "waves." The author suggests a comparison between the oncoming Asians and _____.
    By examining Asian Americans in these terms what are we associating these people with?

4. In what ways have state governments and the media contributed to the spread of anti-Asian feelings?

5. What do the words "both men" on line 48 refer to?

6. What does Zinsmeister suggest are the "personal cost[s]" many successful Asian Americans pay for being successful?

7. Why does Zinsmeister see inner-city resentment of Asian Americans as more serious than the resentment that occurs in small towns?

8. To what do the words "a large number" on line 105 refer?

9. Explain why Zinsmeister says American businessmen are "ambivalent" toward their Asian counterparts.

10. What are the two great superpowers mentioned on line 144?

11. What words in lines 144–146 indicate the author's opinion?

12. Sometimes an author will put an important quote in parentheses behind the name of the person who said it. On line 154, what did Congressman Dingell call Asians?

13. Carefully reread the paragraph between lines 169 and 173. Based on United States population statistics, what percentage of Asian-American freshman students *should* one expect to find on United States campuses?

14. Based on "statistics" in the article, what percentage of Jewish freshman students should one expect to find on United States campuses?

15. What do the words "in this" on line 171 refer to?

16. What does "that" on line 196 refer to?

17. What does "it" on line 198 refer to?

18. What does "that" on line 199 refer to?

19. In the last paragraph, Zinsmeister writes "intolerance will be but a minor part of our problems." What does he imply will be a main part of our problems?

20. Zinsmeister uses subtitles and subheadings to divide his essay into five sections. In your own words summarize, in two sentences per section, each section in the spaces provided below:
    Homegrown Hatreds_____
    _____
    _____

    Black Resentments_____
    _____
    _____

    Prejudice at the Peak_____
    _____
    _____

    College Quotas_____
    _____
    _____

    Anxiety and Acceptance_____
    _____
    _____

21. Summarize this reading selection in 75 to 100 words.

READING #2

Prereading

Directions: These are some of the words that you will need to understand before reading the passage.

not a Chinaman's chance (noun phrase): a racist idiom meaning little or no chance.

to hit (someone) (verbal idiom): to realize.

Vocabulary in Context

Directions: Read the following passage without using your dictionary. As you read the passage, try to guess the meaning of the following words, all of which are underlined in the passage. Write your guesses in the appropriate column and look up the words in an English-English dictionary to check your guesses. Then reread the passage, using your dictionary, and do the exercises at the end of the passage.

Words	My Guess	Dictionary Definition
indignation		
infuriated		
ethnic		
stereotype		
menial		
sanctioned		
barred		

BEING CHINESE IN AMERICA

by Teresa Fung

1   "Well, you're more than qualified, but what would U.S. congressmen think if they saw
2   a foreign face lobbying for American interests?"
3   That was what a Washington, D.C., lobbyist told me last summer when I applied to be
4   an intern with his organization. The <u>indignation</u> did not hit me until later. But when it did
5   I was <u>infuriated</u>.
6   In the recesses of my mind, I still remember the expression on my father's face when
7   he described how someone had yelled at him across a New York City parking lot, "Go
8   home, Chinaman." Or how my best friend in junior high, Susan, assured me that "I
9   consider you American. You just look Chinese."
10   Today, I often wonder when I will no longer have to explain that I speak good English
11 because it is my mother tongue. Or why I am majoring in political science and English, not
12 physics. Or how I can be a U.S. citizen if I am Chinese. My fundamental question is this:
13 When will I be accepted as an American with a Chinese <u>ethnic</u> background and not as an
14 "Oriental" without an accent?

15 **DISTURBING IGNORANCE**

16   As a second-generation Chinese American, I find it disturbing that ignorance about
17 the Chinese still exists in this country. The first Chinese came to America in the late 1700s.
18 They were merchants, laborers, students, and servants. In 1848, some 20,000 Chinese
19 came to mine gold in the streams around San Francisco. In the 1870s, a new wave of
20 Chinese immigrants helped build California's railroads. Like members of many other
21 ethnic groups, Chinese immigrants have continued to seek a better life in this country.
22   Today, there are more than 900,000 Americans of Chinese descent. Chinese Ameri-
23 cans are among the best educated of the nation's ethnic groups. Yet, there are virtually no
24 Chinese in the executive ranks of the top U.S. businesses. What's more, officials at several
25 top U.S. universities have suggested limiting the number of Asians accepted to their
26 schools.
27   Part of the problem is perception. In many ways, Chinese Americans are considered
28 the model minority—a group of intelligent, persevering, achievement-oriented individ-
29 uals. But this very <u>stereotype</u> causes people to resent us. If only more people realized that
30 over 70 percent of Asians in this country hold <u>menial</u>, low-paying jobs in restaurants,
31 clothing factories, and offices.

32   Anti-Chinese sentiments in our country are not new. In the mid-1800s, for instance,
33 signs stating "NO CHINESE NEED APPLY" could be seen throughout California. Mobs
34 ransacked Chinese-owned laundries and homes. Many Chinese were beaten and mur-
35 dered.

36 **PREJUDICE BY LAW**

37   Much of the prejudice against Asians was <u>sanctioned</u> by law. In 1873, the city of San
38 Francisco passed the Queue Ordinance. This law required Chinese men to cut off their
39 traditional long braids of hair, known as queues. In 1882, Congress passed the Chinese
40 Exclusion Act, which <u>barred</u> further Chinese immigration. Another U.S. law prohibited
41 Chinese from testifying in federal courts against white men. That's how the phrase, "not a
42 Chinaman's chance" was born.

43   It would be misleading to say that Chinese Americans face the same type of
44 discrimination today. But prejudice against Chinese Americans—and other ethnic
45 groups—still exists. That prejudice is rooted in ignorance. If each of us would only take
46 the time to find out about people from different ethnic backgrounds, we would destroy
47 the seeds of discrimination.

48   I urge you: Enroll in a Chinese history course. Attend a Chinese cultural event. Get to
49 know a Chinese American in one of your classes. In learning about the rich history of one
50 ethnic group, you'll begin to appreciate all ethnic groups—and what each contributes to
51 the great melting pot which is America.

Teresa Fung was a senior at Oberlin College and a summer intern at *Update* when she
wrote this article.

Reading for Full Comprehension

1. What percentage of Asian Americans have menial jobs?

2. How many Americans are of Chinese descent?

3. When did the first Chinese come to America?

4. The author implies that Chinese Americans are often stereotyped. What is
   that stereotype? Compare the ideas of the author of the first article and those
   of the author of the second article about the effect that this stereotype has on
   other Americans.

5. The author mentions two examples of modern-day social discrimination
   toward Chinese Americans and other Asian-American minorities. What are
   they?

6. When the author writes in lines 11–12 "not physics," what is the author
   implying?

7. Why does the author review the history of Chinese Americans?

8. In the second-to-last paragraph the author uses the words "seeds" and "rooted." She is comparing prejudice and discrimination to _____.

9. What does the author's friend Susan probably believe about the way Americans should look?

10. For whom did the author probably write this article?

    What evidence do you use to make your decision?

11. Summarize this reading selection in 75 to 100 words.

THE MOVIE: DIM SUM

A. What is the relationship between these two people?

B. What ethnic group are these people members of?

About the Movie

Directions: Divide the following passage into phrases and mark the primary stress in word groupings and sentences. Read the passage aloud to a classmate. Have your classmate indicate where he/she heard the phrase divisions and primary stresses. Compare your markings with your classmate's markings.

The movie's first scenes are ones that introduce the three main characters of this drama: Mrs. Tam; Geraldine Tam; and Uncle Tam, the brother-in-law of Mrs. Tam and the uncle of Geraldine.

The first character the viewer meets is Mrs. Tam, who is seen trying to complete a sewing project on the sewing machine in her home located near the Chinatown district of San Francisco. The second character is Geraldine, Mrs. Tam's daughter, who is seen looking out on the water of San Francisco Bay. The third character introduced is Uncle Tam, who is in the process of closing his bar, located in Chinatown.

While he is searching in his pockets, presumably to find keys, he discovers a dim sum, a Chinese pastry, in his pocket and begins to eat it. The movie's plot begins and revolves around the relationships among these three people.

Cultural Points about the Movie

Directions: Read the following passage and discuss the questions at the end of the passage with a small group of your classmates.

Chinese New Year is the most important of all festivals in Chinese societies. It begins on the first moon of the lunar year, which usually falls in the latter part of January or in February. It is a time for family gatherings. Among the customs of the seasons are the following: wearing red, which symbolizes happiness; distributing luck money in red envelopes, which is done by the family's older generation and given to the younger generation, often the children; and setting off firecrackers to scare off the evil spirits.

— — — — —

Dim sum is a Cantonese word which has two meanings. Literally it means "a little bit of heart." However, most often dim sum refers to Chinese pastry. Dim sum comes in a variety of flavors and styles. As you will learn in the film, different kinds of dim sum are associated with different Chinese festivals. For example, in the film the characters make zhong, a kind of dim sum that is associated with the Dragon Boat Festival, which falls on the fifth day of the fifth lunar month.

— — — — —

In the movie, Mrs. Tam becomes a United States citizen. In order to become a United States citizen, one must first pass a very simple examination that includes a section on basic American history.

Discussion Questions

1. How is New Year's celebrated in your country? What special food, clothing, or activities are typical of the New Year in your country?

2. Describe some special holiday foods in your country.

3. What must an immigrant do to become a citizen in your country?

Movie Vocabulary

Directions: Study these words before watching the movie.

cantaloupes (noun): a kind of fruit. Used in the film as a slang term for a woman's breasts.

Dynasty (proper noun): a popular weekly nighttime TV soap opera of the 1980s about the lives and problems of several wealthy families in Denver, Colorado. Alexis was a female lead in this TV drama.

fortuneteller (noun): a man or a woman who is able to see into another's future and predict forthcoming events.

mahjongg (noun): a Chinese game for four players, played with tiles.

to give someone the willies (verbal idiom): to make someone feel scared or nervous.

to Betamax (verbal idiom): to videotape something using a Betamax machine. This is an example of how a noun can be used as a verb. Betamax is a proper noun and technically not a verb. However, here it is being used as a verb.

You can take the girl out of Chinatown, but you can't take Chinatown out of the girl (sentence): this sentence pattern is a common one used to show how one cannot escape the influence of one's environment. The meaning can be changed by inserting the person and the place one wants to make the point about. *For example:* You can take the boy out of the country, but you can't take the country out of the boy.

Discussion Questions

1. Explain to a small group of your classmates any proverb from your language that is similar to "you can take x out of y, but you can't take y out of x."

As You Watch the Movie

Directions: Read the following questions. Keep them in mind while you watch the movie. After the movie, discuss your answers to these questions with a small group of your classmates.

This is a movie about a Chinese-American family, the Tams. Geraldine, the daughter, who has remained at home while her brother and sister have left to start their own lives, is torn between obligation and independence. Her sense of obligation tells her to remain with her elderly, widowed mother and take care of her. At the same time, however, she longs to move away and get married to her long-time boyfriend, Richard.

The situation is further complicated by her mother's belief in the prediction of a fortuneteller who long ago told her she would die at the age of 62, which Mrs. Tam now is. Believing she will soon die, Mrs. Tam plans a trip back to China in order to pay her respects and see the old country.

Meanwhile, Geraldine is left to make a choice. Throughout the drama, we meet Geraldine's friends and relatives and discover how each has adapted to American culture in a particular way.

Postmovie Discussion Questions

1. Director Wayne Wang uses several symbols throughout the film that include the following: the bird cage, the shoes, dim sum, and the garden. What do you think each of these things symbolized?

2. On a continuum place the following characters from the movie according to how assimilated they appear to be: Geraldine, Mrs. Tam, Uncle Tam, Kevin, Amy, Julia, Richard, and Auntie Mary. Explain your choices.

1	2	3	4	5	6	7	8	9	10

Unassimilated   Assimilated

3. How does Geraldine interact differently with her mother, her uncle, her friend Julia, her brother and sister, and her boyfriend Richard?

4. Why are Geraldine and Uncle Tam "similar casualties"?

5. How is Julia's character used as a contrast to Geraldine's character? How is Aunt Mary's character used as a contrast to Mrs. Tam's?

6. Why do you think director Wayne Wang used silence so often in the film?

7. How does the director indicate that Geraldine is very much like her mother?

8. How did Uncle Tam come to learn about American culture?
9. Julia states that her mother purposely waited to die until all her children had left. How does this view of death contrast with Mrs. Tam's perspective on death?
10. What do you think Geraldine will do with her future?

MOVIE REVIEW #1

Prereading

Directions: These are some of the words that you will need to understand before reading the passage.

a cat's cradle (compound noun): a child's finger game of crossed strings.

dead pan (adj.): showing no emotion.

dead on (adj.): honest and without overt sentimentality.

jellies (noun): a type of plastic summer shoe.

Ozu: a Japanese director.

Polaroids (proper noun): pictures taken with a Polaroid instant camera.

to tap (verb): to use, to draw on, to channel.

Vocabulary in Context

Directions: Read the following passage without using your dictionary. After you have
read the passage without a dictionary, try to guess the meaning of the
following words, all of which are underlined in the passage. Write your
guesses in the appropriate column and look up the words in an English-
English dictionary to check your guesses. Then reread the passage, using
your dictionary, and do the exercises at the end of the passage.

Words	My Guess	Dictionary Definition
mosaic		
cronies		
startling		

"Curs" is a root that means "run." "Pre" is an affix that means "before." What do
you think "precursor" means?

A REVIEW OF *DIM SUM*

by Sheila Benson

From: "Calendar," Los Angeles Times, October 16, 1965, p. 5.

1 Director Wayne Wang looks at the Chinese of San Francisco in "Dim Sum: A Little Bit
2 of Heart" in almost exactly the same way Bill Forsyth looks at his fellow Scots in "Comfort
3 and Joy." Dead on, deadpan, with the deepest affection and only the smallest hint of
4 drollery.
5   Neither director explains much; each takes his own time (which, in the case of Wang,
6 can be rather measured), and quiet is the order of the day. Yet the emotion that "Dim
7 Sum" taps is profound. Its pull is both distinctly Chinese and utterly universal: the cat's
8 cradle of obligation/guilt/duty of a concerned child for his or her parent.

9 The principals of this San Francisco-based chamber film are the cheerfully assimi-
10 lated Geraldine Tam (Laureen Chew) and her resolutely unassimilated mother, Mrs. Tam
11 (Kim Chew), who still answers her daughter's comments in Cantonese, even after forty
12 years in America. Victor Wong ("Chan Is Missing," "Year of the Dragon") plays Uncle
13 Tam, the family's "other father," a position he has held since his brother's death fifteen
14 years ago. (The Chews are real-life mother and daughter.)

15 Mrs. Tam, who has been given a cutoff date by a Cantonese fortuneteller (she mustn't
16 expect to live much beyond 62), is approaching that age. Tidily, she plans a last trip back to
17 China to pay her final respects and portions out the family treasures. "This year she's even
18 taken Polaroids of them," Geraldine sighs to her uncle.

19 It's both an ongoing threat and a real worry, to Geraldine and to her friends, many of
20 whose parents are in a faraway "old country."

21 Wang builds his portrait from a mosaic of scenes: Mrs. Tam and her mahjongg
22 cronies, followed by Geraldine and her "m.j." buddies (a precursor of thirty years to
23 come); the predictable dither of family celebrations, which Mrs. Tam describes succinctly
24 to her back-fence neighbor: "Everybody ate and everybody left"; Geraldine with her
25 boyfriend of longstanding, Richard (John Nishio), a doctor in Los Angeles, and a
26 devastatingly funny crack about Chinese men by Geraldine's lovely friend Julia (Cora
27 Miao).

28 Nothing startling occurs, but you may discover that the calm celebration of the
29 everydayness of their lives is seductive. Wang (working with a real budget this time and a
30 fine photographer, Michael Chin) punctuates his scenes with silent still lifes within Mrs.
31 Tam's immaculate house, or glances with sweet tellingness at shoes all in a row in the down
32 stairs hall—orthopedic shoes next to plastic "jellies." It's a rather conscious quote from
33 Ozu, who's also referred to in Terrel Seltzer's screenplay, but it doesn't lose Wang's own
34 steadfast tone.

35 Deaths, decisions and a coming-to-terms are all part of "Dim Sum," but, most of all,
36 the solidity and enduring nature of these characters are revealed. Poignantly. Quietly.
37 With the greatest tenderness.

Reading for Full Comprehension

1. What country does Bill Forsyth come from?

2. What movie did Bill Forsyth make?

3. Did this reviewer probably enjoy Bill Forsyth's movie?

4. By using the words "portrait" and "mosaic" on line 21, the author compares Wang to a _____.

5. T/F   According to the author only Chinese children feel concern for their parents.

6. The reviewer's choice of the words "punctuates" and "a rather conscious quote" in the seventh paragraph indicate the reviewer is comparing the director to a _____.

7. The parenthetical remark in lines 15–16 explains what words in line 14?

8. What other movies has Victor Wong been in?

9. In the second-to-last paragraph the reviewer has written "calm celebration" in the first sentence. What do you think the writer's intention was in putting together two words which seem to suggest opposite meanings?

10. What do we learn about the content of Ozu's movies from the words "It's a rather conscious quote from Ozu" on lines 32–33?

11. The reviewer writes in the fifth paragraph ". . . are in a faraway 'old country.'" What does she mean?

12. In the sixth paragraph the reviewer writes ". . . a precursor of thirty years to come." What does she mean?

13. What does the reviewer mean by the ". . . director [doesn't] explain much" in line 5?

14. Summarize this reading selection in 75 to 100 words.

MOVIE REVIEW #2

Vocabulary in Context

Directions: Read the following passage without using your dictionary. As you read the passage, try to guess the meaning of the following words, all of which are underlined in the passage. Write your guesses in the appropriate column and look up the words in an English-English dictionary to check your guesses. Then reread the passage, using your dictionary, and do the exercises at the end of the passage.

Words	My Guess	Dictionary Definition
burdens		
patent		

Words	My Guess	Dictionary Definition
antecedent		
intimation		

One way to guess the meaning of words is to look for the word "such." When "such" is followed by a noun, as in "such intimations," the definition of the noun "intimations" can be found somewhere in the paragraph before the word "such." Given this, what does the word "intimations" mean?

The Latin root "super" can mean "on the top of." "Fic" means "surface." What does "superficial" mean?

The Latin root "fil" can mean "child." What does it mean for someone to show "filial devotion?"

The Latin root "ante" means before. "Ced" means "coming." Therefore, an "antecedent" is someone or something that _____.

TALES OF TWO CITIES

by Stanley Kauffmann on Films

1   Wayne Wang was born in Hong Kong in 1949, came to the United States in 1967 to
2 study painting, and eventually took a degree in film. After the predictable struggles, both
3 here and back in Hong Kong, after much TV work, he got two American grants totaling
4 $25,000 and made his first feature, "Chan Is Missing," in 1982. It was a black-and-white
5 comedy mystery set in San Francisco's Chinatown, a pleasant film though overrated. Now
6 Wang has made a feature in color—good color, shot by Michael Chin—set in and near the
7 same Chinatown and called "Dim Sum." The title is too cute and is irrelevant, even though
8 those appetizers are made and eaten in the film, but in technique and intent the second
9 feature is a far advance over the first.
10   Wang's great asset is his people; he not only knows Chinese Americans, he knows the
11 performers to represent them winningly. The screenplay by Terrel Seltzer is about as
12 banal as possible: a young woman is trapped by <u>filial</u> <u>devotion</u> into caring for her ailing
13 mother so that she can't marry and move away with the man she loves; but all the actors
14 provide flavors that make them interesting even when they are arguing or reconciling at

15 the most <u>superficial</u> level of international domestic drama. Laureen Chew, the daughter,
16 Kim Chew, her mother, and Victor Wong, as the brother of the deceased head of the
17 family, are engaging human beings, able to suggest matters more profound than anything
18 they are given to say or do.

19   What <u>burdens</u> the film more heavily than the script is that Wang has chosen a lofty
20 model, the Japanese master Yasujiro Ozu. (Even if it weren't otherwise <u>patent</u>, there's an
21 overt reference to Ozu in the script.) Wang falls naively into an old snare; out of
22 admiration, he imitates style and thinks that he thus achieves both the style and the
23 substance of which the style is only a part. One <u>antecedent</u>: for a few years after
24 Antonioni's first impact, some young filmmakers thought that if they made pictures that
25 moved slowly, they were making Antonioni films. Here Wang apparently believes that if
26 he shows shots of empty rooms and of bustling streets in between the script's scenes of
27 action, he is reaching Ozu dimensions. He even shows us shots of shoes, like the shoes
28 outside the hotel door in "Tokyo Story," along with a shot of a seated man and woman
29 facing the sea as in that film. What is missing is any iota of what Ozu creates in those
30 "empty" shots, the conviction that the world in which his characters live is a leading
31 character in their drama. The empty rooms and the bustling streets become just an artsy
32 way to deal with the old chore of filmmaking, the time lapse.

33   If Wang had done his film without grandiose overlay, it wouldn't have been any
34 deeper, but the method would have been less of a handicap to his actors. In Ozu, we are
35 made to feel that the actors understand and are part of the whole film; no such <u>intimation</u>
36 here. This is soap opera, split up with stasis. Wang knows the subleties and complexities of
37 Chinese-American life. Perhaps next time he'll address them without pretense.

Reading for Full Comprehension

1. What sentence in the first paragraph suggests that the reviewer may be critical of this film?

2. What do the words "second feature" in lines 8–9 refer to?

3. What two elements of the movie does Kauffmann review in the second paragraph?

4. How does the reviewer define "old snare" in line 21?

5. Does Kauffmann believe *Dim Sum* is a better film than *Chan Is Missing*?   Yes/No   In what line do you know this?_____

6. In what way does Wang imitate Ozu? In what way is he unlike Ozu?

7. What are some examples of shots from Ozu's movies?

8. In the third paragraph the reviewer mentions the impact of Antonioni on young filmmakers. By giving this example, what comparison is he strengthening?

9. By using the words "predictable struggles" in line 2, what is the reviewer saying about Wang's experiences as a director as compared with those of other directors?

10. What is another word in line 21 that means the same as "patent"?

11. What is the reviewer's *general* opinion of the cast?

12. Summarize this reading selection in 75 to 100 words.

WRITING ASSIGNMENTS

1. According to the article "Anxiety over Asian Americans," there is tension between Asian and African Americans in many large American cities. Describe the tension and explain its causes. Cite information from the article.

2. At the end of the film, we are not certain what Geraldine will do with her life. Imagine you are a friend of Geraldine's. She has written you a letter explaining her dilemma and asking for your opinion and advice. Write a letter to her explaining what you think she should do and why she should do it.

3. Describe and critique the symbolism of the bird cage, the garden, the dim sum, and the shoes in the movie. For each symbol, write one paragraph describing it and another explaining its storytelling function.

4. Write a movie review for your school newsletter. In the first paragraph give your opinion of whether the movie is worth watching and support your opinion with some *general* opinions of the actors, the script, etc. Then, in your second and third paragraphs explain your opinions in more detail.

5. Imagine a friend asks you "What is *Dim Sum* about?" In sixty words or less, summarize the plot *and* the purpose of *Dim Sum*. To help you summarize the purpose, it might be helpful for you to try answering the question, "Why did Wayne Wang make this movie?"

6. Contrast Uncle Tam's assimilation into American culture with Mrs. Tam's. You may choose either to write first on Uncle Tam's assimilation then on Mrs. Tam's and then to contrast the two, or to select three to four areas where their assimilation differs and after introducing an area show how Uncle Tam and Mrs. Tam's assimilation contrast in that area.

7. In the movie, Uncle Tam says he learned about American culture through American movies. After watching *Dim Sum*, what have you learned about the differences between Chinese and American culture? Determine three or four cultural differences. (Your introductory paragraph should contain a

thesis sentence that mentions each of the differences.) Write a separate paragraph to explain how each difference is shown in the movie.

8. Write a paper in which you describe for a foreigner two or three of the family obligations that are expected of young adults in your country. Your thesis sentence should identify these obligations and should be followed by paragraphs detailing these obligations.

9. Using information from the first two articles, trace the history of *legislative* and *governmental* discrimination against Asian Americans in one paragraph. In a second paragraph, explain how this discrimination has changed over the years. Is it now more or less obvious? Is it now more or less severe? Explain your opinion on these questions using information from the two articles.

10. Have you ever been torn between a cultural obligation or tradition and the desire to do what you wanted to do? If you have, describe and explain how you dealt with this conflict. (Two to three pages in narrative form.)

11. Describe an experience you have had with prejudice or discrimination. (Two to three pages in narrative form.)

6

SO, WHAT ABOUT THE CHILDREN?

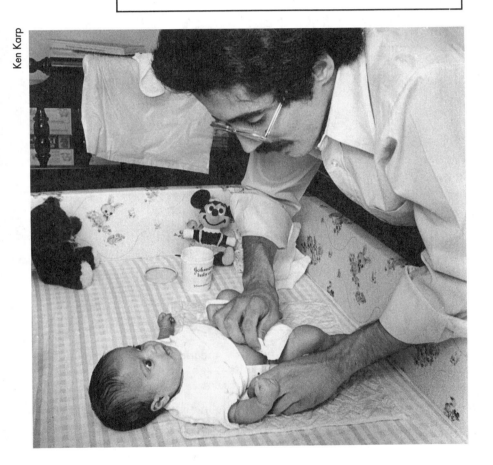

A. Why do you think this man is diapering a child?

B. Do you think he enjoys what he is doing?

C. Do men in your country do this? If so, when?

INTRODUCTION

Vocabulary in Context

Directions: Read the following passage without using your dictionary. As you read the passage, try to guess the meaning of the following words, all of which are underlined in the passage. Write your guesses in the appropriate column and look up the words in an English-English dictionary to check your guesses. Then reread the passage, using your dictionary, and discuss the reading with your classmates.

Words	My Guess	Dictionary Definition
custody		
gender		
entailed		
domain		

The Latin root "nata" means birth. The prefix "pre" means "before." Based on there roots, what kind of information do you think might be taught in prenatal classes?

1 With one out of every two American marriages ending in divorce, divorce has become
2 a reality for many American families who just a generation ago thought "it will never
3 happen to us." Up until the late 1970s, it had been common practice in the United States
4 automatically to award <u>custody</u> of children to the mother when a divorce occurred.
5   However, since the 1970s, this practice has been slowly challenged. Most custody
6 battles today are decided, in theory, on the basis of who is the more fit parent and on what
7 is in the child's best interest—not on the <u>gender</u> of the parents. The reality, nevertheless, is
8 that most women still win custody of their children when it is an issue in a divorce.

9   This legal change was an outgrowth of the social changes that took place in the United
10 States during the 1960s and 1970s. The social changes <u>entailed</u>, among other things,
11 challenging many of the traditional roles men and women were expected to play. As a
12 consequence of this challenge, it is not uncommon nowadays to find women working
13 outside their homes and being as concerned about their careers as they are about their
14 personal lives. It is also not uncommon to see men accepting roles that were once
15 considered the exclusive <u>domain</u> of women, such as taking care of their infant children in
16 public; shopping for groceries; driving their children to and from school; cleaning their
17 homes; and even accompanying their wives to <u>prenatal</u> <u>classes</u> and helping out in the
18 delivery room. To hear men openly discussing the need to bond with their children and to
19 be seen by their children as nurturing parents is also not unusual anymore.
20 Because of the increase in the divorce rate, the change in the roles that men and
21 women are expected to play, and the changing attitudes of the judicial system toward child
22 custody, more men have started to fight for and win custody of their children when
23 divorce occurs.

Reading for Full Comprehension

1. What does the passage imply were the traditional roles of men and women?

2. How many American marriages end in divorce?

3. Why do you think the writer of this passage wrote "in theory" on line 6?

    What phrase does the writer use to contrast with "in theory"?

4. What are the three factors that have caused men to fight and win custody of their children, according to this passage?

5. T/F   The author would agree that legal changes can be both the cause and the effect of social changes.

READING #1

Prereading

Directions: These are some words that you will need to understand before reading the passage.

a constant balancing act (noun phrase): a constant struggle to keep things in order or to keep a situation stable.

assertiveness training (compound noun): a type of psychological training designed to help people to assert their basic rights.

a Jewish mother (noun phrase): refers to a mother, not always Jewish, who shows a great concern for, is overly protective of, and is heavily involved in her childrens' lives.

a meal ticket (noun phrase): someone or something that will provide one with the means to survive.

Archie Bunker (noun): a TV character of the 1970s who was known for being a stereotypical working-class male.

blue collar (adj.): relating to one who engages in physical labor.

Brody bunch (noun phrase): a play on "Brady Bunch," which was the name of a popular TV show in the early 1970s about a widow with three daughters who married a widower with three sons.

Brownie (noun): the first level of Girl Scouts, a girls' organization.

dear old dad (noun phrase): a term of endearment for a father.

dress-for-success manuals (compound noun): books that tell one how to dress to succeed in business.

heavy-duty (adj.): when it relates to a physical object it means strong and durable. When it relates to an action it means serious and involved.

in snapshot terms (adv.): in a quick, visual way.

Jaguar (noun): a type of sports car.

Kramerization (noun): the process of a father, often single, realizing his paternal responsibilities and his nurturing nature. Taken from the movie *Kramer vs. Kramer*.

nuts and bibs (noun phrase): a play on the idiom "nuts and bolts" which means the central elements of an issue. The word "bibs" is used here instead of bolts because a bib is part of every baby's wardrobe.

self-improvement movement (noun phrase): a fashionable way to improve oneself economically, physically, socially, or psychologically (e.g., in the 1970s, jogging was a popular self-improvement movement).

third-string quarterback (noun phrase): a quarterback is a position on a football team. A third-string quarterback is one who is on the third team, which means his position is not an important one.

to buck the system (verbal idiom): to challenge or oppose a system.

to hold a candle to (verbal idiom): to compare favorably to; often used in the negative (e.g., does not hold a candle to).

to jog up the fast track (verbal idiom): to make an effort to advance in ones position, especially in business.

to pay lip service to (verbal idiom): to support something in words but not in actions.

to work oneself to death (verbal idiom): to work oneself to exhaustion or to death.

turf (noun): a piece of land; someone's area of expertise.

Vocabulary in Context

Directions: Read the following passage without using your dictionary. As you read the passage, try to guess the meaning of the following words, all of which have been underlined in the passage. Write your guesses in the appropriate column and when you have finished reading, look up the words in an English-English dictionary to check your guesses. Then reread the passage, using your dictionary, and do the exercises at the end of the passage.

Words	My Guess	Dictionary Definition
befell		
peripheral		
revision		
fixation		
draw		
bristle		

Words	My Guess	Dictionary Definition
infringement		
trend		
egalitarianism		
tended		
adept		
forebears		
cradling		
paces		
misconstrued		
neophytes		
coped		

Words	My Guess	Dictionary Definition
rapport		
domesticity		
to wobble		
favored		
stigmatized		
loath		
own up to		
yearnings		
juggle		
render		
prodded		

As you know, the Latin root "pater" means father. What do you think "paternal involvement" means?_____

If "maternity leave" is time-off given to working women after the birth of a child, what is "paternity leave"?_____

A NEW KIND OF LIFE WITH FATHER

by Lynn Langway with Lisa Whitman in New York, Marsha Zabarsky in Boston, John Carey in Chicago and bureau reports

From: *Newsweek*, November 30, 1981, © Newsweek, Inc. All rights reserved. Reprinted by permission.

1   If Frank Nemzer fantasized about fatherhood before it befell him, it was strictly in
2 snapshot terms: dear old dad scorches hamburgers in the backyard or plays catch with the
3 kids. "My virgin assumption was that fatherhood was largely a titular job," says Nemzer,
4 34, a social-security administrator from Staten Island, N.Y. "Dad got all the good parts: go
5 to work, earn money, enjoy the children. Was I surprised!" With two children and a wife
6 who works, Nemzer has learned that fatherhood can be a full-time occupation. Instead of
7 fiddling with his beloved old Jaguar, he now devotes most nights to cooking dinner and
8 shampooing and bathing his children, and he skips sports-car rallies to attend Brownie
9 outings. "Sure, life is a constant balancing act," he says, "but that's part of the deal."
10   In a culture that has traditionally regarded the raising of children as primarily the
11 mother's concern, it is very much a new deal—and while it is a long way from universal, it is
12 being struck in an increasing number of American households. Spurred by changing
13 social mores, as well as simple economic necessity, growing legions of men are rejecting the
14 notion that father is the peripheral parent. And as they face up to both the pleasures and
15 pains of child rearing, they are discovering that dad can be just as caring as mom—and
16 might even enjoy it. "Men have always had a need to be tender and to nurture," says
17 pediatrician Lee Salk. "Now society is allowing it to emerge."
18   This revision of family relations has led to something of a fatherhood fixation,
19 particularly among relatively affluent younger men. How-to books about "parenting" are
20 becoming as sought after as dress-for-success manuals, while "fathering" classes spon-
21 sored by hospitals and child-care clinics are jammed with men who want to learn how to
22 diaper and dandle their infants. Prenatal workshops now draw nearly as many prospective
23 fathers as mothers, and many dads-to-be chat knowledgeably about "bonding" with their
24 newborns by helping out in the delivery room. "Fatherhood is the new family romance of
25 the '80s," says New York psychiatrist Avodah K. Offit. "It's the unexplored frontier."

26   Passionate paternal involvement is still a long way from being the norm, particularly
27 in bastions of blue-collar machismo. Content—or caught up—with their traditional role as
28 family provider and protector, many men still <u>bristle</u> at doing what they consider to be
29 "women's work" as well. Similarly, many mothers resist what they regard as an <u>infringe-</u>
30 <u>ment</u> on their turf. And even where both parties are willing, unsympathetic employers
31 may balk at pleas for special considerations, such as paternity leaves.

32   But the <u>trend</u> is clear. These days, nearly 60 percent of the nation's mothers with
33 children under 18 work outside the home—and according to a recent survey of 1,500
34 American families by the General Mills food conglomerate, eight out of ten men agree that
35 when both parents work, "mothers and fathers should play an equal role in caring for the
36 children." (Such <u>egalitarianism</u> doesn't necessarily extend to housework. A 1980 survey by
37 the Benton & Bowles advertising agency found that about half the men with working
38 spouses were willing to share responsibility for cooking and cleaning.)

39   **Similarities:** What's more, a steadily climbing divorce rate has combined with
40 changes in child-custody laws to create a rising new class of single fathers. According to the
41 1980 census, more than 1 million children are now raised exclusively by their fathers, a 65
42 percent increase since 1970. Single fathers are still vastly outnumbered by single mothers.
43 But the burgeoning of the role—beautified by movies such as "Kramer vs. Kramer"—has
44 helped to discourage the idea that mother always knows best.

45   A growing body of research certainly indicates that mothers are not the only
46 caretakers who count. In one series of studies, for example, Harvard psychologist Milton
47 Kotelchuk showed that infant emotional needs can be satisfied equally well by either
48 parent; when upset, the babies he studied turned for comfort to whichever parent most
49 often <u>tended</u> them. "Both parents seem to care equally and seem equally <u>adept</u> at reading
50 clues about the baby's needs," says University of Texas psychologist Douglas Sawin.
51 Indeed, adds psychologist Ross Parke, who has observed the behavior of mothers, fathers,
52 and babies over the last ten years, "we find that the similarities much outweigh the
53 differences."

54   Men who plan to share child rearing usually get involved long before their wives give
55 birth. Increasingly, when she becomes pregnant he enrolls along with her in childbirth
56 classes, where he learns how to time her contractions and pace her breathing in the
57 delivery room. "Prenatal participation used to be considered unmanly," says Elizabeth
58 Bing, whose pioneering childbirth classes have seen male enrollment double in the last ten
59 years. "Now it's not only accepted, it's expected." Some expectant fathers get so involved in
60 their wives' pregnancy they suffer sympathy pains, nausea, and weight gain—known as
61 the Couvade Syndrome, after the French "couver," to hatch. "The assumption that fathers
62 are irrelevant during pregnancy is completely untrue," says Dr. Alan Gurwitt, a psychia-
63 trist who teaches at the Yale Child Study Center.

64   The strongest lifelong bonds between parents and children seem to be forged in the
65 delivery room—and the increasing involvement of men in that crucial experience may be
66 the signal difference between the new generation of fathers and its <u>forebears</u>. As late as
67 1970, most U.S. hospitals did not permit a father to be present at the birth of his child; now
68 men are encouraged to take part. Several recent studies show that when they are involved
69 in the birth, fathers often feel "engrossment"—an enduring emotional link with the child
70 once thought to be exclusively maternal, that is fostered by immediate physical contact
71 with the newborn. "To be in the labor room and to be able to take an active role—I

⁷² wouldn't trade that for anything in the world," says actor Ron Howard, 27, the boyish star
⁷³ of "Happy Days," who was at his wife Cheryl's side when she gave birth to their daughter,
⁷⁴ Bryce, eight months ago. "I've been in a lot of exciting situations, with thousands of people
⁷⁵ carrying on, but that doesn't hold a candle to being there when this person popped out."

⁷⁶   **Nuts and Bibs:** After the delivery-room high, some fathers find caring for the infant
⁷⁷ at home a definite downer that they would prefer to skip. "Our culture gives a father lots of
⁷⁸ excuses for not dealing with a crying or messy baby," says Richard Bell, who teaches a
⁷⁹ popular course on "Father and His Baby," at St. John's Hospital in St. Paul, Minn. But the
⁸⁰ nuts-and-bibs instruction provided by courses like Bell's encourages many papas to
⁸¹ persevere—that is, assuming they can overcome maternal resistance. "For some men, the
⁸² class was their first legitimate excuse to be alone with their children," says Bell, who
⁸³ stopped scheduling classes for mothers next door because the women would come in and
⁸⁴ take charge when the babies fussed. "Just as women needed assertiveness training in the
⁸⁵ workplace, men needed assertiveness training at home," says Steve Bogira, a father and
⁸⁶ freelance writer who started a "nurturant fathers" group in Chicago. Without encourage-
⁸⁷ ment, he says, "guys get pushed to the sidelines like a third-string quarterback."

⁸⁸   But more and more fathers are refusing to be benched. "It never occurred to me not
⁸⁹ to be involved," says Rafael Yglesias, cradling his six-month-old son, Matthew, against his
⁹⁰ shoulder as he paces his Manhattan apartment on long, tireless legs. Yglesias, 27, a
⁹¹ successful novelist and screenwriter, shares child-raising duties with his wife, Margaret, a
⁹² magazine art director. "I thought the early period would be the most boring, that the
⁹³ interesting part would come when Matthew was older and able to talk," he says as he
⁹⁴ cuddles the gurgling infant. "But there is an immediate, overwhelming, instinctive
⁹⁵ response in seeing a small baby. I would have felt very alienated if I'd had to go to an office
⁹⁶ nine hours a day and then come home to find my wife involved in this new process by
⁹⁷ herself. I would have felt estranged."

⁹⁸   Such close paternal involvement benefits children in many ways. Studies by Ko-
⁹⁹ telchuk and others indicate that kids who are frequently cuddled and cared for by their
¹⁰⁰ fathers wind up better able to withstand stress and adapt to outsiders; they also seem to
¹⁰¹ learn more easily. "So many of our social problems are related to paternal deprivation,"
¹⁰² says psychologist Henry Biller of the University of Rhode Island. Ironically, many fathers
¹⁰³ fear that displays of affection will be misconstrued as sexual overtures or "sissified"
¹⁰⁴ behavior. In fact, the reverse is probably true; many experts say that close, loving fathers
¹⁰⁵ help to establish a sense of sexual identity and security in both boys and girls.

¹⁰⁶   **Neophytes:** There had been little research into father-daughter relationships, but
¹⁰⁷ studies of successful women do indicate that they often had strong, supportive fathers. "If
¹⁰⁸ a woman has a good relationship with her father, she has a better chance of understanding
¹⁰⁹ men emotionally and succeeding in a career," says psychotherapist Roberta Chaplan, who
¹¹⁰ runs father-daughter workshops at New York's Hunter College.

¹¹¹   No man is more involved with his children than the single father. Just four years ago,
¹¹² Edwin Lynch, 39, became the first father in Massachusetts to win custody of a child, and he
¹¹³ remembers his "Kramerization" well. Until his divorce, he recalls, he lived the unliberated
¹¹⁴ life of the old Archie Bunker: "I'd come home and have a beer. When supper was ready,
¹¹⁵ I'd eat. After supper, I'd go down to my workshop, putter around, and yell if the kids
¹¹⁶ made too much noise." After his marriage ended, however, he won custody of his 10-year-
¹¹⁷ old daughter, and confronted the mysteries of the ironing board. "She used to wear these

118 little pleated skirts with scorch marks," he recalls wryly. To help other <u>neophytes</u> master
119 household skills, single fathers like Lynch have banded together in support groups
120 around the country—and a small magazine, "Single Dads' Lifestyles," advises 2,000
121 readers about everything from removing gum from children's hair to explaining menstru-
122 ation.
123   For chemical engineer Stan Brody of Houston, Texas, single fatherhood happened
124 virtually overnight. Four years ago, his wife—a full-time homemaker—died, leaving
125 Brody, 51, with a 3-year-old girl, twin 5-year-old boys and a 7-year-old son. He <u>coped</u> by
126 curtailing his business travel and his social life. Still, he says, his Brody bunch offers full
127 compensation whenever he comes home. "All the children wait for me by the door and
128 they gang up on me. It's such a real expression of love. I don't think I ever realized before
129 how very much I love my children."
130   But single fathers aren't the only men who choose to be the primary parent. A small
131 but increasing minority of married men are deliberately taking on that role. Mainly, they
132 are educated professionals, married to women who earn good salaries. Some become full-
133 time househusbands, like Michael Scott Peterson, 33, a former college basketball star and
134 accountant who now does chores and cares for two young children while his wife works as
135 a public-relations executive. At first Peterson felt estranged from his neighbors. "All these
136 women had something in common to talk about—their pregnancy, what it was like to carry
137 their child," he says. But he eventually managed to establish playground <u>rapport</u>.
138   For all its emotional rewards, full-time fatherhood can be economically draining.
139 Peterson reports that he and his wife have found that they are able to save more money
140 now than when both worked and had to pay for day care. But other at-home fathers say
141 that some sacrifices are inevitable. "It has to be hurting my career," says freelancer Bogira.
142 "But I've exchanged the benefits of the outside world for the benefits of the hearth." Still,
143 resentment sometimes flares as men discover the painful job-family conflicts that women
144 have known for years. "I often wonder how much money I could be making if I weren't in
145 the laundry room folding clothes," says Ray Lovett, a Washington psychoanalyst who
146 divides his time among seeing patients, writing, and caring for his two sons, while his wife
147 works full-time as a clinical psychologist.
148   **Parental Balance:** Yet some men take to <u>domesticity</u> with astonishing passion—and
149 ease. Until two summers ago, Bill DeBord was jogging up the executive fast track at
150 Caterpillar Tractor Co., earning $83,000 a year in salary and benefits as a European-based
151 sales representative. "I was the father who was always loving and always away," says
152 DeBord, 34. "When my son was a year old, he thought the houseman was his father." That
153 hurt—so DeBord quit his job, moved the family back home to Peoria, Ill., and set up a food
154 wagon selling pasta and hot dogs with his wife, a former systems analyst, in the shadow of
155 Caterpillar's corporate headquarters. "A lot of my co-workers come by every day," he says.
156 "Some of them think I'm crazy, but a lot of them say they admire my courage." Son
157 Nathan, 3, and daughter Oriana, 1, are always nearby, and DeBord admits no regrets. "My
158 father literally worked himself to death," he says, "so I believe the most important thing
159 you can give your children is your time."
160   Few families go quite that far. The general goal seems to be parental balance. In
161 Meriden, Conn., for example, salesman Dennis Nolan, 31, makes a point of coming home
162 for lunch so he can play with his seven-month-old daughter, Abby. He also gets up at 6
163 A.M. on weekends to spend time alone with her. "He's heavy-duty involved," beams wife

164 Avery. Musician Rob Wasserman of Mill Valley, Calif., tries to compensate for his
165 frequent road trips by making an extra effort when he's home: he dresses daughter Sara,
166 6, makes her lunch, takes her to and from school and brings her along to his rehearsals.
167 "I'm the Jewish mother in this family," he smiles. And Wesley Jameson, 34, has chosen to
168 work a night shift as a cargo serviceman so he can see his two daughters by day. Wife
169 Earline takes over in the evening. "To raise children properly, I think both parents really
170 need to be with them," Jameson says. "Otherwise, children have a way of getting away
171 from you."
172   The fatherly spirit is transforming some very traditional households. Until Bob
173 Bondick was laid off from his foreman's job in Dearborn, Mich., last fall, he'd never seen
174 any of his five children take their first step. But he was there the day baby Diana finally
175 managed to wobble across the living room floor—and he was overjoyed. "You never
176 imagine how good it is to be with the kids every day and get them to know you," says
177 Gondick, who hopes to reform his workaholic ways when he lands another job. Robert
178 Mullenix, an Atlanta, Ga., banker, has gradually become more involved with his two
179 children—and reached "the 50–50 point" with his wife over the last five years. "I began to
180 realize that I had to change and meet her halfway," he says. "If there's a conference at
181 school, I take time to go, and I see a lot of fathers there—I guess they must feel that way,
182 too."
183   Perhaps the biggest problem for men who want to do more with their children is that
184 employers rarely make it easy for them. According to a recent study of 1,300 major
185 corporations made by Catalyst, a career think tank for women, few companies pay more
186 than lip service to the idea of paternal participation. More than 80 percent of the
187 executives surveyed acknowledged that men now feel more need to share child-raising
188 responsibilities—but nearly 40 percent also agreed that "realistically, certain positions in
189 my firm cannot be attained by a man who combines career and parenting." While a quarter
190 of the companies said they favored the idea of paternity leaves, fewer than one in ten
191 actually offered them. "We talk about working mothers, but not working fathers," says
192 day-care consultant James Levine. "Men are still stigmatized when they take on a
193 traditional female role, even if that's what they want to do."
194   **Choices:** Whatever their feelings, relatively few fathers do buck the system. Even
195 when the boss is sympathetic, men may not want to sacrifice salary or face: few, for
196 example, have taken the six-month unpaid paternity leave that AT&T has been offering
197 its employees since 1979. And when they do take time off to be a father, many men are
198 loath to admit it, finding it safer to say they were writing a book rather than minding a baby
199 when they want to re-enter the job market. The reluctance to own up to paternal yearnings
200 reflects more than just job strategy. "The fear of losing the self-respect involved in earning
201 money, more than any other factor, keeps men from sharing in parenting on a full-time
202 basis," says full-timer Lovett. "I'm an ambitious man, and I've always wanted the same
203 things that other men want—success, prestige, and income. But you can't have it both
204 ways. Everybody pays a price for the choices he or she makes."
205   Yet society is beginning to recognize that fathers and mothers have choices—however
206 difficult when it comes to parental roles. "Women have moved over and left space for
207 males in the home," says sociologist Frank Furstenberg of the University of Pennsylvania.
208 As more women juggle jobs and family, more men are shifting their priorities, too,
209 refusing excessive relocations, or workloads that would render them absentee parents.

210 "You're seeing male reaction against workaholism," says Queens College sociologist
211 Cynthia Fuchs Epstein. "A man wants to be more than a meal ticket."
212   To be sure, the 50–50 family is still unusual, and both social and personal forces will
213 probably keep it that way for years. But—whether they're <u>prodded</u> by their wives, pressed
214 by divorces, or simply seeking more emotional warmth—more men are looking for close-
215 up fatherhood. "We are in a period of vast transition," says psychoanalyst Offit. "Instead
216 of repeating their fathers' mistakes, men desperately want to learn how to do better." That
217 search won't stop, predicts S. Adams Sullivan, father of two and author of "The Fathers'
218 Almanac." "This is not just a passing trend," he says. "Fathers are being forced into closer
219 relationships with their children . . . and then falling in love." Somewhere in the midst
220 of America's latest self-improvement movement, many fathers are finding joy. "Most men
221 have denied themselves this pleasure," says Ray Lovett. "It's a powerful feeling: my hand is
222 on the cradle with my wife's."

Reading for Full Comprehension

1. What kind of activities did Frank Nemzer <u>think</u> fathers participated in?

2. What does "it" on line 1 refer to?

3. What are the two basic reasons given in paragraph 2 to explain why more fathers are becoming more involved in parenting?

4. T/F   The article implies that wealthier men care more for their children than do poorer men.

5. According to the fourth paragraph, even if a man wants to get involved with his children, what two individuals might resist his efforts?

6. T/F   80 percent of men agree that mothers and fathers should take equal care of the children and do equal parts of the housework.

7. Approximately how many children lived with single fathers in 1970?

8. T/F   Recent research studies indicate fathers are better at caring for children than mothers are.

9. Look up the words "high" (on line 76) and "downer" (on line 77). The author is comparing early childhood parent/child interaction with_____ .

10. What are sympathy pains?

11. Look up any of the following words that you don't know: "sidelines" (line 87); "third-string quarterback" (line 87); "benched" (line 88). The author is comparing male involvement with _____ .

12. On line 95, the author says "I would have felt very alienated . . ." What is another word in the same paragraph that means the same as "alienated"?

13. What is meant by a 50–50 family?

14. List the reasons men give for choosing to stay at home.

15. What are two of the regrets, the writers of this article mention, that fathers have about full-time fatherhood?

16. What are the two factors that have combined to create an increase in the number of single fathers, according to this article?

17. T/F   It can be inferred that 40 percent of major United States corporations do not permit men who combine parenting and careers to advance as far as men who do not combine the two.

18. Look up the meaning of the word "face" on line 195. Find another word in the same paragraph that means the same thing.

19. With the exception of the first and last paragraph and one example paragraph in this article, each paragraph has a clearly stated topic sentence appearing in either the first or second position in the paragraph. Find these topic sentences. Underline them.

20. Do these twenty-one sentences provide a complete summary of the article? Yes/No   What kind of information do these sentences not provide?

21. Summarize this reading selection in 75 to 100 words.

READING #2

Prereading

Directions: These are some of the words that you will need to understand before reading the passage.

good dad/bad dad (noun phrase): good x/bad x is a way of showing strong contrast between two people.

male chauvinist (noun phrase): a man who believes in the superiority of men over women.

Snugli (noun): a cloth device worn on the chest to hold a small child.

to be on the books (verbal idiom): to be legal; to be a law.

to bring a toothbrush (verbal idiom): indicates one will not be going home to sleep so one should come prepared to stay.

welfare-reform bill (noun phrase): a law to improve government services to children or the poor.

Vocabulary in Context

Directions: Read the following passage without using your dictionary. As you read the passage, try to guess the meaning of the following words, all of which have been underlined in the passage. Write your guesses in the appropriate column and when you have finished reading, look up the words in an English-English dictionary to check your guesses. Then reread the passage, using your dictionary, and do the exercises at the end of the passage.

Words	My Guess	Dictionary Definition
upheaval		
imposed		
compliance		
advocates		
predominantly		
plummets		
intractable		
noncustodial		

AND WHAT OF DEADBEAT DADS?

by Pat Wingert with Patricia King

1   There is a flip side to the nurturing father who walks around with a Snugli on his
2   chest. He is the father who just walks away. Some 5.6 million children under the age of 15
3   live in homes without a father today. Only one third receive financial support from their
4   fathers. The same social <u>upheaval</u> that loosened traditional sex roles enough to allow
5   fathers to get closer to their children also permitted others to take no responsibility for
6   supporting the children they father. Some never marry the mothers of their children;
7   others stop support after separation or divorce. It's the "Good Dad/Bad Dad" phenome-
8   non, says sociologist Frank Furstenberg of the University of Pennsylvania.
9   More than half of the men ordered by a court to pay child support pay less than
10 required or nothing. The amount of child support is generally so low that most of these
11 children live in poverty. Recently, Congress decided to do something about the problem of
12 deadbeat dads. The welfare-reform bill passed this fall includes a little-publicized provi-
13 sion, to be <u>imposed</u> over the next six years, that should mean bigger and more dependable
14 child-support payments for many families. Once the bill is in full effect in 1994, payments
15 will be taken out of the noncustodial parent's paycheck automatically. Amounts would be
16 determined by state standards, not by a judge's discretion. That discretion has meant
17 average payments as small as $10 a week in states like Alabama, according to Geraldine
18 Jensen, founder of the Association for Children for Enforcement of Support, a Toledo,
19 Ohio, based group with chapters in thirty-seven states.
20 Jensen considers the new law a step in the right direction but has her doubts about its
21 enforcement. Garnishment of wages has been on the books for years, she reminds, yet
22 "only 23 percent of the child support due in 1987 was actually paid." She also notes that in
23 a recent federal audit, thirty-five states were found not to be in <u>compliance</u> with federal
24 child support laws.
25 Fathers' rights <u>advocates</u>, meanwhile, argue that the laws are too one-sided. Women
26 who violate court-ordered visitation decrees routinely escape punishment. But deadbeat
27 dads are far more likely to face jail sentences. Says Chicago attorney Jeffrey Leving: "If I
28 go to court with a man who hasn't paid child support, I'd better bring a toothbrush for
29 him." Some men drop out of their children's lives not out of cruelty but because they feel
30 divorce decrees leave them with little or no say in how the kids will be raised. Divorce
31 courts are "archaic, adversarial, and have a strong maternal preference," says James Cook,
32 president of the Joint Custody Association, a Los Angeles-based parents' rights group.
33 "The militant feminists were correct. Judges are <u>predominantly</u> male chauvinists." Cook

34 says the deadbeat rate <u>plummets</u> when fathers are given equal time and equal say in the
35 lives of their children.
36   Whether or not the judges and politicians are to blame, getting the fathers involved
37 won't be easy, says Penn's Furstenberg: "The most <u>intractable</u> problem stems from the fact
38 that many, if not most, <u>noncustodial</u> fathers are only weakly attached to their children." A
39 1981 study of the National Survey of Children found that nearly half of all children
40 between the ages of 11 and 16 living with their mothers hadn't seen their fathers in a year.
41 "There is a small group of fathers who are trying to do it all," he says, "and a much larger
42 group of men who are doing very little."

Reading for Full Comprehension

1. According to the article, the loosening of traditional sex roles has provoked two reactions in fathers. What are they?

2. How many children are living in homes without fathers?

3. T/F   Less than 2 million children who live apart from their fathers receive financial support from them.

4. What are the different ways mentioned in paragraph number one that fathers fail to take responsibility for their children?

5. According to the article, how many states do not follow federal laws regarding child support?

6. T/F   If all fathers who were supposed to pay child support did so, their children would not live in poverty.

7. What are the two effects the new welfare-reform bill will have on child-support payments?

8. T/F   Currently, judges set the amount of child-support payments.

9. Why do some fathers not take an interest in their children's lives?

10. Why does James Cook make the charge that "judges are predominantly male chauvinist"?

11. On line 41, it says, "There is a small group of fathers who are trying to do it all." To whom does this refer? Give examples from the article.

12. Underline the topic sentences in each of the five paragraphs of this article.

13. Summarize this reading selection in 75 to 100 words.

THE MOVIE: KRAMER VS. KRAMER

A. What do you think is the relationship between these two people?

B. What meal are they eating?

C. Who makes the meals at your house? Does your father prepare food?
   If so, what foods does he prepare?

About the Movie

Directions: Listen as your teacher dictates this passage. Draw a line (|) where your teacher pauses. Draw dots (·) over words that receive primary stress. Draw a checkmark (✔) over the word that gets the heaviest stress in the sentence.

The movie starts as advertising executive Ted Kramer has just been told by his company's vice-president that if he does well on a new advertisement campaign, he will receive a promotion. That same evening, Ted comes home late, after celebrating with his boss, to find his wife Joanna preparing to leave him. At first he thinks she is not serious, but soon he realizes she is going to leave him and their son Billy. She leaves that night. The next morning Ted Kramer begins his life as a single father with his son Billy.

Cultural Points about the Movie

"Kramer vs. Kramer" literally means Kramer versus (against) Kramer. The term "vs." is used in legal action when one party sues or brings legal action against another party. The last names of the two parties are used.

Movie Vocabulary:

Directions: Study these words before watching the movie.

Burberry raincoat (noun phrase): a brand of raincoat.

con artist (noun phrase): someone who attempts to con, to cheat, another person.

hot shot (noun phrase): someone who is an expert at something and shows off that expertise.

Madison Avenue (noun phrase): a street in New York where most of the major New York advertising agencies are located.

open and shut (adj.): clear and already decided.

schlock (noun): from Yiddish, meaning someone or something of low class.

the guys upstairs (noun phrase): the important leaders or bosses in an organization or corporation.

the writing on the wall (noun phrase): a clear sign or indication of something.

to beat the pants off (verbal idiom): to clearly and forcefully beat an opponent.

to bring home the bacon (verbal idiom): to bring home money to support a family.

to get into therapy (verbal idiom): to receive psychotherapy.

to get the show on the road (verbal idiom): to start an action.

to give someone a shot (verbal idiom): to give someone a chance.

to give them a tap dance (verbal idiom): to make a sales pitch to someone; to try to persuade someone to do something.

to play your cards right (verbal idiom): to do the right things.

to take one's stripes (verbal idiom): to demote a person.

Women's Lib (noun phrase): The Women's Liberation movement is a movement organized to fight for and advance women's rights.

As You Watch the Movie

This is a movie about how an individual, Ted Kramer, changes and grows as a person and father. As you watch the movie, consider how Ted Kramer develops as a father, a friend, and a person. Specifically, consider how he relates to his son, Billy; his neighbor; and Joanna, his wife, at the beginning of the movie and how he relates to them by the end of the movie.

Postmovie Discussion Questions:

1. When we first see Ted Kramer, is he portrayed as a good husband?

2. Why does Joanna not want to return to the apartment when she and Ted are arguing in the hall at the start of the movie?

3. How does the director show the type of father Ted Kramer has been at the beginning of the movie?

4. What does Ted's cleaning the house of Joanna's things symbolize?

5. Why do you think Billy behaves the way he does after he receives his mother's letter?

6. Why did Joanna leave?

7. One technique directors use to show change is to show a scene two or more times with slight variations in the action. For example, the director of this movie shows Ted Kramer making breakfast three times. What change does each scene show?

   What change is shown in the three elevator scenes?

   What change is shown in the scenes where Ted brings Billy to school?

8. How do you think the ice-cream eating incident contributes to the growth of the father-son relationship?

9. In court, how does Joanna explain leaving her child?

10. Does Joanna seem surprised by the changes in Ted during his testimony?

11. What does Joanna's comment about not painting clouds reveal?

12. What do you think will happen to Joanna, Ted, and Billy in the future?

MOVIE REVIEW #1

Prereading

Directions: These are some words you will need to understand before reading the passage.

a must (a modal made into a noun): something that is necessary.

conscience of the community (noun phrase): the attitude or belief of a community about something.

court of appeals (noun phrase): a court where one is able to appeal (to ask to be overturned) a previous decision.

people oriented (adj.): a person who likes interacting with other people.

to jump a hedge (verbal idiom): to overcome a barrier.

Wicked Witch of the West (noun phrase): a character, a witch, in the movie "The Wizard of Oz" who was very evil and mean. Used to describe someone with these characteristics.

Vocabulary in Context

Directions: Read the following passage without using your dictionary. As you read the passage, try to guess the meaning of the following words, all of which have been underlined in the passage. Write your guesses in the appropriate column and when you have finished reading, look up the words in an English-English dictionary to check your guesses. Then reread the passage, using your dictionary, and do the exercises at the end of the passage.

Words	My Guess	Dictionary Definition
hustling		
testified		
split up		
rearing		
champions		
inclined		
adjustments		
endorsement		

Words	My Guess	Dictionary Definition
grumps		
concedes		
statute		
enacted		
abdicates		
meticulously		

CUSTODY: KRAMER VS. REALITY
In divorce cases, as in society, rules are changing

---

1   While moviegoers have been weeping this winter over the wrenching divorce drama
2 "Kramer vs. Kramer," lawyers have been shaking their heads. Their complaint is not that
3 the couple's attorneys in the film are the least appealing characters since the Wicked Witch
4 of the West, but that the courtroom scenes are legally out of date. Meryl Streep, playing a
5 restless housewife trying to find fulfillment, has walked out on her marriage to Dustin
6 Hoffman, a hustling young Manhattan adman, leaving him with their young son; eighteen
7 months later she wins custody of the child despite the husband's devotion to the boy
8 during her long absence. In the real world, psychiatrists or psychologists would have

9 testified, the judge would have at least interviewed the child and probably would have
10 allowed the father to retain the custody he had since the split-up.
11   More and more, single dads are rearing their children. While women still get custody
12 in the overwhelming majority of divorces, between 1970 and 1978 the number of children
13 under 18 living with divorced fathers jumped by 136 percent; close to 500,000 divorced
14 U.S. fathers are now rearing sons and daughters without the help of a wife. At the same
15 time, many other ex-spouses are trying another fast-spreading arrangement: joint cus-
16 tody, in which fathers and mothers share the responsibilities for the rearing of their kids.
17   In Roman times and after, the man was king: offspring were considered his property
18 even if the marriage ended. That principle died in the nineteenth century as courts took
19 on a guardian role and began to favor the mother, especially if the child was in his first five
20 to seven years. The rule that generally prevails in the U.S. today—that custody must be
21 based on the "best interests of the child"—was articulated in a landmark decision in 1925
22 by Benjamin Cardozo, then a New York State Court of Appeals judge. Though the rule is
23 sex-blind in principle, men seldom win custody in the 10 percent of the cases that go to
24 court. "The courts are prejudiced against fathers," insists Leonard Kerpelman, a Bal-
25 timore lawyer who champions fathers' rights. "Unless the mother is a prostitute, a drug
26 addict, or a mental defective, she is automatically assumed to be the better qualified to have
27 custody."
28   While many judges cling to this "unfitness" test, things are changing. The emergence
29 of job-holding mothers (59 percent of women 18 to 64 now work) has eliminated a leading
30 legal basis for favoring the ex-wife. Fathers, encouraged by the new emphasis on equal
31 rights, are increasingly inclined to put up a fight.
32   . . . Once a father has obtained custody, whether by agreement or by court ruling,
33 he faces lots of adjustments. If his work hours are a problem, he may have to find a new
34 job. Most single fathers rely on female friends or parents to help; day care is often a must.
35 Yet most appear to cope and find the sacrifices worthwhile. Says Brandeis University
36 sociologist Kristine Rosenthal: "It is very interesting to see what it does to a man to pay the
37 kind of attention to children that women usually do." Her study of 130 single dads showed
38 that they became "more people-oriented" and less concerned about work.
39   One endorsement comes from Sidney P. Harden of Columbus, Ga., a printer who
40 works for a company producing Hallmark cards. Harden, 26, assumed custody of his son,
41 now 3½, in September. Though he grumps that his new life "has not been very exciting,"
42 he concedes that he has "grown up a lot. I can take care of my son just like his mother
43 could. Now I love my son twice as much." Such good feelings, Rosenthal says, are shared
44 by many sole-custody fathers. One told her: "I actually made dinner for my kid, instead of
45 taking him to McDonald's, and he really liked it!"
46   Some advocates of divorce-law change believe that only joint custody makes sense.
47 Says Garry Brown, former head of Equal Rights for Fathers of New York State: "I don't
48 care how inadequate a parent is, a kid is entitled to his two loving parents." Brown favors a
49 system under which the child lives with one parent, while the other has unlimited visitation
50 rights and a full voice in decisions involving the child's rearing. On January 1, California
51 became the fourth state (after Oregon, Iowa, and Wisconsin) to adopt a statute specifically
52 providing the option of joint custody. Although the other forty-six states have not enacted
53 such laws, they do permit parents to ask for joint custody.

54 While few lawyers quarrel with the goals of joint-custody advocates, many question
55 the wisdom of this arrangement. "It's the easiest thing for a judge to decide," says Family
56 Law expert Henry S. Foster, Jr., professor emeritus at New York University Law School.
57 "He then abdicates his responsibility. The judge represents the conscience of the commu-
58 nity; he should meticulously examine all the facts from the perspective of the child and
59 then decide." Of course, such an arrangement can succeed only if the parents are able to
60 work out details harmoniously, a hedge that can be tough for a warring couple to jump. If
61 nothing else, an amicable joint-custody agreement usually costs less than a full-scale battle
62 for sole custody; few lawyers blinked at the moment in "Kramer" when Dustin Hoffman
63 was told that his legal bill would be at least $15,000.

Reading for Full Comprehension

1. What are the two basic complaints about the movie that the author mentions in the first paragraph?

2. A common conditional pattern in English is the past conditional:
    If that had been the case, he would have done it.
    The "if" clause is often reduced or eliminated entirely:
    In that case, he would have done it.
    What "if" clause has been reduced/eliminated in the sentence that begins on line 8?

3. What does "that principle" on line 18 refer to?

4. What percent of custody cases are actually fought in court?

5. What do the words "this 'unfitness' test" on line 28 refer to?

6. Read the sentence on lines 28–30 carefully. What was one of the major reasons that courts used to favor the ex-wife?

7. Explain how joint-custody arrangements usually work.

8. What does the word "a hedge" on line 60 refer to?

9. Summarize the legal history of child custody practices discussed in this article.

10. What is the author's purpose for writing that the 1925 law dealing with child custody is "sex blind in principle"?

11. What are some of the sacrifices the author tells you are made by many single fathers?

12. What did the author mean when he said "few lawyers blinked . . . [when Kramer's] legal bill . . . [came to] $15,000," line 63?

13. Summarize this reading selection in 75 to 100 words.

MOVIE REVIEW #2

Prereading

Directions: These are some words that you will need to understand before reading the passage.

after-school pickup (compound noun): when someone picks up children after school, it is called an after-school pickup.

Blondie cartoon (noun phrase): a popular cartoon about a traditional couple called Blondie and Dagwood.

Dagwood (noun): Dagwood is Blondie's sometimes stupid husband.

inkblot test (compound noun): a psychological test that is given to determine what people can perceive from a series of ink images.

in the same boat (adverbial): in the same situation; having the same experience.

off-beat (adj.): that which is not conventional.

one liner (compound noun): a joke which is one line.

to be a natural (verbal idiom): to have a natural talent to do something.

to founder on the rocks (verbal idiom): what happens to an object when it is washed ashore and hits the rocks.

to play it for cuteness (verbal idiom): to appeal to that which is cute or overly sentimental.

to come of age (verbal idiom): to reach maturity.

Vocabulary in Context

Directions: Read the following passage without using your dictionary. After you read the passage, try to guess the meaning of the following words, all of which are underlined in the passage. Write your guesses in the appropriate column and look up the words in an English-English dictionary to check your guesses. Then reread the passage, using your dictionary, and discuss the reading with your classmates.

Words	My Guess	Dictionary Definition
dispensed to		
plight		
tandem		
dissolves		
protagonist		
rendered		
counterfeit		
bumbling		

<u>Words</u>	<u>My Guess</u>	<u>Dictionary Definition</u>
boundaries		
clichés		
imbued		
elusive		
alimony		
sullies		
ennobling		
unremitting		

KRAMER VS. KRAMER VS. THE WAY IT IS

by Gene Lichtenstein

From: *Atlantic,* March 1980, pp. 96–98.

1   Maybe I should start by saying that I have been divorced, have been a "single parent,"
2 and, moreover, have worked, as a psychologist and therapist, with people in the same boat.
3 All of which made me a natural for the film "Kramer vs. Kramer," even without the
4 advance publicity; so I went with considerable expectations. The film, directed by Robert
5 Benton and starring Meryl Streep and Dustin Hoffman, had been praised lavishly by both
6 *The New Yorker* and *New York* magazine, had been the recipient of a glowing *Time* cover
7 story and a glowing *Newsweek* cover story, had been acclaimed by the *New York Times* in a
8 review and in a profile of Dustin Hoffman, and had been approved by my weekly
9 alternative newspaper, the Boston *Phoenix*. Unlike the reviewers, however, I left the
10 theater irritated, even angry.
11   Why the critics' unreserved praise? Part of their enthusiasm, I suspect, was occasioned
12 by the star presence of Meryl Streep and Dustin Hoffman. She clearly had an extra-
13 cinematic role as media personality of the year, appearing everywhere (in films, theater,
14 and magazines), while his story came under the heading of Star Makes Comeback. And to
15 some extent, the attention was related to Robert Benton's role as director. More than ten
16 years ago, he wrote "Bonnie and Clyde," with David Newman; later he directed an
17 imaginative and beautifully constructed film, "Bad Company," and then went on to write
18 and direct the offbeat comedy "The Late Show." His films have tended to be wry and
19 ironic, almost literary; but the two films he directed were box office failures. And while the
20 critics had liked his work, they had not until now singled him out for the kind of publicity
21 and favor they had <u>dispensed to</u> other directors.
22   But part of the reason for their attention is undoubtedly the subject matter of
23 "Kramer vs. Kramer": divorce and the <u>plight</u> of the single parent, in this instance, the
24 single male parent. The statistics are boring, but presumably one out of every two
25 marriages ends in divorce, and in California, so the joke goes, the casualty rate has jumped
26 to three out of every two. Divorce, new roles for men and women, adaptation to modern
27 life, these are the issues now confronting many in the middle class. That's where the
28 changes are taking place; that's where the action is.
29   Like most revolutions, this one proceeds in <u>tandem</u> with all the older forms and ways
30 of doing things. So, for example, many divorces are handled the way they have been
31 during the past forty years; there are just more of them. Similarly, many judges (and
32 couples) still assume that the mother is the logical parent for child custody when a family
33 <u>dissolves</u> (though California and five other states no longer automatically make that

34   assumption), and joint custody arrangements are a solution for only a minority of
35   divorced couples nationally. But they are the couples, by and large, who give shape to the
36   cultural class that embraced Dr. Lamaze and natural childbirth twenty years ago and
37   consciousness-raising for women and men during this past decade. They are readers of
38   *New York* and *The New Yorker, Time* and the *New York Times* and even of the Boston *Phoenix*
39   and its counterparts in New York and elsewhere. I, of course, like thee, am part of it to
40   some degree or other, willingly or not. And it is they—we—who devour all culture, mass to
41   avant-garde, who adapt the new trends and styles as they come off the latest magazine
42   page, and who help create them as well. It is no accident, for example, that in "Kramer vs.
43   Kramer" the <u>protagonist</u> is an art director in an advertising agency, and not, say, an
44   insurance agent or a factory worker (just as the star of "An Unmarried Woman" works in
45   an art gallery and the abandoned husband in "Starting Over" is a writer). For Dustin
46   Hoffman's problems in the film, divorce and coping with being a single parent, are
47   presented in terms of cultural style. It is a beautifully <u>rendered</u> style (the film's first
48   conversation concerns the social implication of a Burberry raincoat), but our sympathies
49   for the man depend too much on our identification with the details of his wardrobe,
50   menus, verbal habits.
51   The film's inner movement is the change that is wrought in the behavior and
52   character of the single parent, who is altered because he allows himself to attend to his
53   seven-year-old son, accepting the nurturing role that he and we have heretofore defined
54   as mothering. The change itself, Ted Kramer's coming of age, is a moving one. But the
55   path to that change, so artfully rendered by quick vignettes and the director's perceptive
56   eye for details, seemed to me rather <u>counterfeit</u>.
57   Let me give some examples. In one of the early scenes, Ted Kramer tries, during his
58   first morning as 'the' parent, to prepare breakfast for his son, Billy, while getting the boy
59   ready for school and himself off to work. He starts with an air of forced geniality, but in
60   rapid order everything turns chaotic. He mixes the French toast batter in a coffee cup,
61   burns the breakfast, grabs for the hot frying pan with his bare hand, and drops pan and
62   French toast on the floor. It is a funny 1970s version of the old Blondie cartoon, with
63   Dustin Hoffman playing Dagwood, the <u>bumbling</u> but well-intentioned husband.
64   That scene is followed in rapid succession by other cartoon sequences. Kramer and
65   Billy in the supermarket demonstrating Ted's unfamiliarity with shopping and culminat-
66   ing in a clever one-liner; Ted Kramer's night of sex, ending with Billy and Ted's nude
67   girlfriend meeting en route to the bathroom in the early morning hours; Ted's <u>boundaries</u>
68   scene, in which he forbids Billy to eat ice cream until dinner is finished and, when tested,
69   permits himself to lose his temper and punish the boy, thereby giving in to his own feelings
70   and showing that he really cares for his son; Ted's presence at school during the
71   Halloween play, the only man among all the mothers, coaching Billy from the audience,
72   involuntarily, when the boy forgets his lines; and, finally, the climactic scene when Ted
73   sees his son fall from the top of a jungle gym in Central Park and dashes, the boy cradled in
74   his arms, to Lenox Hill Hospital, where, over the doctor's objections, he insists on being
75   present while the stitches are sewn into Billy's face.
76   That last scene particularly bothered me. In itself, it was authentic and powerful; the
77   pain and fright of the child, the fear and guilt and rush of love of the parent, evoked in all
78   of their dramatic intensity. It is a central scene in the film, for it marks the emotional
79   conversion of Ted Kramer from self-absorbed, ambitious careerist to caring parent. My

⁸⁰ difficulty with it was that little before it had led me to expect a genuine, three-dimensional
⁸¹ response from Ted Kramer. Where had this person come from? Certainly not from the
⁸² film I had been watching. For the incidents that led up to his conversion, that are
⁸³ compressed and sketched in so cleverly, are little more than <u>clichés</u>: situations oversim-
⁸⁴ plified, characters stereotyped, the whole reduced to what Herbert Gold once described as
⁸⁵ "Happy Problems for Happy People."

⁸⁶   How could someone, you ask, be characterized as having "happy problems" when he
⁸⁷ loses his wife, his job, and his child? Easy. In place of his wife he realizes his potential,
⁸⁸ becomes a person, learning to love his son and to empathize with a close friend who is
⁸⁹ herself lonely and abandoned. In place of a job where his boss is brittle and uncaring and
⁹⁰ where the values are tinsel, he settles for a more modest position at less money, but in an
⁹¹ advertising agency where the creative director looks you in the eye and gives you a firm,
⁹² human handshake. And though his son is taken from him by an impartial and nasty
⁹³ judicial system, he regains both his son and the friendship of his wife, for she returns the
⁹⁴ boy to Ted. In the process Ted Kramer, his wife, Joanna, and all of us in the audience are
⁹⁵ <u>imbued</u> with the love and humanity and virtue that at times seems so <u>elusive</u>. For the
⁹⁶ audience, there are truly "happy problems"—the kind that make you glad to be sad.

⁹⁷   What "Kramer vs. Kramer" actually offers us is a portrait of the ideal divorce and the
⁹⁸ ideal parent. Consider what does not happen. Neither parent belittles the other to their
⁹⁹ son. Neither one exhibits jealousy, behaves outrageously, or tries to hold onto or pursue
¹⁰⁰ the other. Instead, each parent matures and becomes better able to function once
¹⁰¹ separation and divorce occur. Nothing like <u>alimony</u> or child support <u>sullies</u> the divorce;
¹⁰² there are no battles over money. Except for Ted's brief display of anger when Joanna says
¹⁰³ she wants custody of the child, the feelings of one toward the other are affectionate and
¹⁰⁴ caring; in fact, they are downright <u>enobling</u>. It is a fantasy divorce, to which many
¹⁰⁵ divorcing couples may aspire, but few experience.

¹⁰⁶   Nor are family life and parenthood any less idealized. Ted Kramer's frustrations
¹⁰⁷ come under the "poor dad" comic-strip heading, and his sacrifices, the loss of a job and of
¹⁰⁸ the possibility of a vice-presidency, we realize are no losses at all. That firm, that boss, that
¹⁰⁹ life, survive, we are shown, only at the death of feeling. He gives up death and is rewarded
¹¹⁰ with life. After it is a life with some of the more tedious domestic details missing. There are
¹¹¹ no babysitters, no day care, no cleaning lady or man, no mundane hours on the telephone
¹¹² arranging for after-school pickup or who will play with whom at whose house. On a deeper
¹¹³ and more pervasive level, there is no sense of the enclosed, <u>unremitting</u> quality of parental
¹¹⁴ life, particularly when the other partner has moved beyond easy commuting distance.

¹¹⁵   What's absent in "Kramer vs. Kramer," ultimately, is any sense of conflict for a parent,
¹¹⁶ and the real choices that he or she makes by giving priority to parenting over career, or
¹¹⁷ over anything else. The film's handling of sex is perhaps the best example of this. Most
¹¹⁸ single parents of Ted Kramer's age and class spend a considerable amount of time
¹¹⁹ thinking about another partner, or reaching out for one, particularly when it is they who
¹²⁰ have been abandoned. Their conflicts are very real ones, often poignant. There is the
¹²¹ matter of "dating" again; of sex, on either a casual or an ongoing intimate basis; of ego and
¹²² self-esteem; and always, there is the matter of the "new" triangle, the way that the child
¹²³ responds to the parent's playmate, lover, or roommate. The anguish and the relationships
¹²⁴ that have foundered on that triangular rock are themselves stories for a film. All I looked

125 for was some recognition of the effect of the new setup on the emotional life of parent and
126 child.
127   Instead, "Kramer vs. Kramer" takes the situation and plays it for cuteness: the date,
128 embarrassed, trying to conceal her nudity, desperately attempting to think of something
129 to say; the boy apparently unaware of anything untoward and talking to her in a natural
130 way about things on his mind; and the father clapping hand to forehead in the bedroom,
131 sliding under the covers. 'Yipes' you can hear him say in a cartoon caption. Amusing. End
132 of sex as an issue. Such a portrait falsifies an experience, a condition of life, that we need to
133 comprehend more fully. Presumably, for many parents, the rewards are worth the price.
134 But it needs to be stated that the stresses in the family life of single parents, of women as
135 well as men, are often acute, always complex, and rarely without high cost. That cost can be
136 measured in terms of career (adjusted), responsibility (total), and freedom (curtailed). By
137 the same measure, the pleasure and pull of family life, the love of children and parents for
138 one another, often become more intense because of the stress, the cost, and not inciden-
139 tally, the absence of another adult. At times, the single-parent life for some adults leads to
140 great depression. They hold on to that role out of a mixture of love and honor, sometimes
141 out of their own dependence, and in some cases because they have no other choice, finding
142 it preferable to abandoning their child. Little, if any, of this dimension is present in
143 "Kramer vs. Kramer."
144   Yet it is precisely because parenthood is such a mixed blessing, precisely because
145 parenting carries such a high price, precisely because the powerful pull of love that an
146 adult feels for a child prevails for some parents over other equally strong attractions, that it
147 has such value. My feelings throughout "Kramer vs. Kramer" were that somehow
148 important experiences were being dismissed.
149   The film is not without its accomplishments. The details create such a textured
150 surface of authenticity, the images, like some rich inkblot or Thematic Aperception Test
151 card, seem so familiar and affecting, that we are quick to provide the story and the
152 background of the characters ourselves. We recognize Ted Kramer instantly as someone
153 familiar to us. It is almost like reading a short story by Irwin Shaw or John O'Hara. We
154 know all the characters by their style, by the places they eat lunch, by the ties they wear in
155 particular settings, by the kitchens they create and the clichéd phrases they use. But
156 American films, as opposed to American novels and American plays, seem to have both an
157 easier and a more difficult time of it when dealing with the complexities of contemporary
158 life. The "easier time," of course, comes from the director's ability to capture class, setting,
159 and identity visually so that we know the characters simply by seeing them. When the
160 director's eye and sensibility are refined and witty, the effects can be charming; when he or
161 she is truly gifted, they can be dazzling. The difficulty, however, is that in film the story
162 often becomes reduced to details that correspond in some dictionary sense to the
163 contemporary "social problem," with characters flattened into engaging stereotypes, all in
164 the service of realism. This may be an inevitable fact of life, given the industry's
165 multimillion-dollar budgets and the need for a mass audience. The result, though, is that
166 our most important social dilemmas get obscured and trivialized by sentimentality.

Reading for Full Comprehension

1. How many magazines and other newspapers are mentioned in this review?

2. What three factors mentioned in the second paragraph contributed to the praise that reviewers gave this movie?

3. Look up the words "casualty rate" on line 25. By using these words the author compares divorce to _____.

4. T/F   The author would agree that most divorces today are different from divorces in 1950.

5. What are some of the other activities that couples who choose joint custody participate in?

6. T/F   The author would probably agree that a factory worker would not be as sympathetic to Ted Kramer as an artist would be.

7. Between lines 57 and 75 the author mentions several scenes from the movie as examples. What is the topic sentence of this section?

8. Why does the author use a question in line 81?

9. What is the purpose of the question on line 87?

10. Between lines 98 and 102, the author mentions many things that didn't happen in the Kramer divorce. Why does he do this?

11. Between lines 117 and 132 the author discusses the way the movie handles the issue of sex. What is the point the author is making by giving this example?

12. On line 124 the words "that triangular rock" refer to _____.

13. What are the three reasons single parents hold on to their role?

14. What are the reasons why parenthood has such value? (See lines 144–147).

15. In the last paragraph the author summarizes the good and bad points of the film. What is the best point of the film? What is the weakest point of the film?

16. What does "this" on line 164 refer to?

17. On line 165, the author writes "the result." What is the cause of the result?

18. Summarize this reading selection in 75 to 100 words.

WRITING ASSIGNMENTS

1. Write a response to the second review "Kramer vs. Kramer vs. Reality" defending the realism of the movie. (Two page composition.)

2. How does the director portray the mother in this movie? What is your opinion about her portrayal? (Two page composition.)

3. What role does Mr. Kramer's neighbor serve in the movie? (Two page composition.)

4. In your opinion, how does Ted Kramer change during the course of the movie? Using examples to back up your opinion, write a two- to three-page composition.

5. Why do you think Mrs. Kramer gives up custody of her son at the end of the movie? Use both the reasons she articulated and any reasons, you may feel, which were not articulated. (Two- to three-page composition.)

6. State your opinion about the behavior of the child in the film. Is the behavior similar to the behavior of children in your country experiencing a like situation? How is it different? What do these differences indicate about social norms of your country and the United States? (Three-page composition.)

7. In your country, when a divorce occurs, how is child custody determined? Explain what cultural norms influence child-custody laws in your country. (Two- to three-page composition.)

8. Are there deadbeat fathers in your country? If there are, how are they treated? (Two-page composition.)

9. Consider your own father's abilities. Do you think he could have taken over your mother's work? (Three-page composition.)

10. What kind of father or mother are you or do you want to be? Or, would you want to be a full-time father or married to a full-time father? State your opinion and reasons in a three-page composition.

7

THE FACE OF RURAL POVERTY

Paul Conklin/OEC

A. How would you describe these people?

B. Where do you think they live?

C. Are large families common in your country?

INTRODUCTION

Vocabulary in Context

Directions: Read the following passage without using your dictionary. As you read the passage, try to guess the meaning of the following words, all of which are underlined in the passage. Write your guesses in the appropriate column and look up the words in an English-English dictionary to check your guesses. Then reread the passage, using your dictionary, and do the exercises at the end of the passage.

Words	My Guess	Dictionary Definition
ravaged		
succumbed to		
respiratory		
ailment		
afflicts		
inhale		

"Pover" is a Latinate root meaning "poor." "Im" is a prefix that can mean "to make." What then is an "impoverished area"? Has an impoverished area always been this way?

———————————————————

1 Appalachia is the forgotten fuel belt of the United States. A mountainous region that
2 extends along the Eastern seaboard of the United States, it is an area rich in coal.
3 As this country developed industrially, it was the Appalachian coal miner who kept it
4 going. Many of them worked long, hard hours in the coal mines in very dangerous
5 conditions. They were, and continue to be, heroes of the Industrial Revolution. They
6 worked the mines that fed the factories that built the nation.
7 Today, Appalachia is one of the most <u>impoverished</u> areas of the United States.
8 <u>Ravaged</u> by generations of mining, its people have been largely forgotten. Many of the
9 coal miners have <u>succumbed</u> <u>to</u> Black Lung Disease, a <u>respiratory</u> <u>ailment</u> that <u>afflicts</u>
10 people who <u>inhale</u> coal dust.
11 Yet Appalachia's people remain a proud people with a unique cultural contribution to
12 make to the United States. This chapter should give you some ideas of their culture, their
13 lives, and their future.

Reading for Full Comprehension

1. What does "it" on line 2 refer to?

2. Take the words "it was" out of line 3, and restate the sentence grammatically. What does the word "it" refer to?

3. What is another word for "region" in the first paragraph?

4. T/F   Appalachia is an area that includes several states.

5. T/F   The Industrial Revolution would not have been possible in America without the people of Appalachia.

6. T/F   The author implies that coal mining is as important today as it once was.

READING #1

Prereading

Directions: These are some words that you will need to understand before reading the passage.

[to] broaden horizons (verbal idiom): to provide an opportunity for something.

company towns (compound noun): towns built and controlled by individual companies.

counterculture movement (compound noun): a popular movement of the 1960s. It emphasized a rejection of urban American culture and a return to a simpler way of life.

down-home folk (noun phrase): simple, rural people.

Mountain State (compound noun): another name for the state of West Virginia.

new ethnicity (noun phrase): a term for a popular attraction to and emphasis on American ethnic minorities.

the Third World (noun phrase): developing countries.

turn of the century (noun phrase): around the time of 1900.

Vocabulary in Context

Directions: Read the following passage without using your dictionary. As you read the passage, try to guess the meaning of the following words, all of which are underlined in the passage. Write your guesses in the appropriate column and look up the words in an English-English dictionary to check your guesses. Then reread the passage, using your dictionary, and do the exercises at the end of the passage.

Words	My Guess	Dictionary Definition
notion		
bolstered		
synonymous		
implicit		
fabricate		

<u>Words</u>	<u>My Guess</u>	<u>Dictionary Definition</u>
alter		
inclusion		
burgeoning		
emergence		
exploit		
plunged		
strife		
concentration		
dislodge		
ranks		

"Bene" is a Latin prefix meaning "good." "Vol" is a Latin root meaning "will." What then does "the benevolence of the employer" (lines 130–131) mean?

INDUSTRIALIZATION AND SOCIAL CHANGE IN APPALACHIA: A LOOK AT THE STATIC IMAGE

by Ronald D. Eller

Condensed from: Ronald D. Eller, *Miners, Millhands, and Mountaineers: Industrialization of the Appalachian South, 1880–1930* (Knoxville: University of Tennessee Press, 1982).

1   We Americans have faith in progress. Throughout most of our history we have
2 assumed that the present is better than the past and that the future will be better still. This
3 reassuring <u>notion</u> is periodically <u>bolstered</u> by statistical evidence of rising production and
4 other measures of improvement in our standard of life. Progress, we believe, is occurring,
5 and the future holds yet unrealized possibilities.
6   Since the late nineteenth century, our idea of progress has become intertwined with
7 the concept of modernity. We have come to believe that progress means technological
8 development, industrial expansion, and growth in material wealth. Modernization has
9 become <u>synonymous</u> with progress, and we tend to measure the improvement of any
10 nation, society, or region in terms of its modernization. "Backward" and impoverished
11 areas like Appalachia and the Third World are thought to exist because of a lack of
12 modernization. The forces of growth and development appear to have passed by these
13 regions. They seem to have been set off by history or geographic isolation from the rest of
14 our progressive world.
15   The belief that time and geography somehow set the southern mountains off from
16 the rest of the American experience has been part of our understanding of Appalachia for
17 almost a hundred years. As early as the 1870s, writers for the new monthly magazines
18 which flourished after the Civil War had begun to develop and exploit a literary image of
19 the region.
20   <u>Implicit</u> in this literary image was a sense of otherness that not only marked the region
21 as "a strange land inhabited by a peculiar people" but defined that strangeness in terms of
22 the process of American historical growth. Because metaphor was more interesting than
23 reality, the Appalachian present came to be linked with the American past, and eventually
24 the analogy was accepted as fact.
25   Succeeding generations have periodically rediscovered and reinterpreted the region
26 in the context of their own day, but the static image has remained the standard perception
27 of mountain life. More recently, the rise of the new ethnicity and the counterculture
28 movement have brought attention to the mountain people as just plain "down-home folk,"
29 and a flourishing minor industry has developed to <u>fabricate</u> such oddities as dulcimers,
30 quilts, log cabins, and "Hillbilly Chicken." Of late, we have also seen the introduction of

31 courses in Appalachian studies and the proliferation of symposia aimed at diagnosing the
32 "unique" qualities of mountain life. But this revival of interest has done little to <u>alter</u> our
33 traditional views. According to one leading student of the region, Appalachia can still be
34 seen "as a vanishing frontier and its people as frontiersmen, suspended and isolated, while
35 the rest of the country moves across the twentieth century."[1] Marooned on an island of
36 hills, the mountaineer has seemed shut off from the forces that have shaped the modern
37 world. He has lived, we are told, in a land "where time stood still."[2]

38   Cast in the static role, mountain people have thus rarely appeared as conscious actors
39 on the stage of American history, and almost never on center stage. They are acknowl-
40 edged to exist somewhere in the background, as subjects to be acted upon, but not as
41 people participating in the historical drama itself. As a result, our efforts to explain and
42 deal with the social problems of the region have focused not on economic and political
43 realities in the area as they evolved over time, but on the supposed inadequacies of a
44 pathological culture that is seen to have equipped mountain people poorly for life in the
45 modern industrial world. Having overlooked elements of movement and change that
46 have tied the mountains to the rest of the American experience, we have blamed the
47 mountaineers for their own distress, rather than the forces which have caused it.[3]

48   Ironically, it was during the same years that the static image was emerging as the
49 dominant literary view that a revolution was shaking the very foundations of the mountain
50 social order. In Appalachia, as in the rest of the country, the decades from 1880 to 1930
51 were years of transition and change. What had been in 1860 only the quiet backcountry of
52 the Old South became by the turn of the century a new frontier for expanding industrial
53 capitalism. The coming of railroads, the building of towns and villages, and the general
54 expansion of industrial employment greatly altered the traditional patterns of mountain
55 life and called forth certain adjustments, responses, and defenses on the part of moun-
56 taineers. This transformation varied in scope and speed, but by the end of the 1920s, few
57 residents of the region were left untouched by the industrial age.

58   The effects of this transition were great. Mountain agriculture, for example, went
59 into serious decline. While the size of the average mountain farm was about 187 acres in
60 the 1880s, by 1930 the average Appalachian farm contained only about 76 acres, and in
61 some counties the average was as low as 47 acres.[4] This decline occurred throughout the
62 region but was most pronounced in the coal fields and other areas of intense economic
63 growth. Significantly, while the total number of farms increased during these years, the
64 total amount of land in farms actually decreased almost 20 percent as a result of the

[1] Cratis Dearl Williams, "Heritage of Appalachia," address to the Southern Appalachian Regional Conference (13 May 1974), reprinted in *The Future of Appalachia* (Boone, N.C., 1975), 128.

[2] Bruce and Nancy Roberts, *Where Time Stood Still: A Portrait of Appalachia* (New York, 1970).

[3] See Dwight Billings, "Culture and Poverty in Appalachia: A Theoretical Discussion and Empirical Analysis, *Social Forces* 53 (Dec. 1974), 315–23; Stephen L. Fisher, "Folk Culture or Folk Tale: Prevailing Assumptions about the Appalachian Personality," in J.W. Williamson, ed., *An Appalachian Symposium: Essays Written in Honor of Cratis D. Williams* (Boone, N.C., 1977), 14–25; David S. Walls, "Internal Colony or Internal Periphery? A Critique of Current Models and an Alternate Formulation," in Helen M. Lewis, et al., eds., *Colonialism in Modern America: The Appalachian Case* (Boone, N.C., 1978), 319–50.

[4] U.S. Department of Interior, Census Office, *The Tenth Census: 1880, Agricultural Statistics*, III; U.S. Department of Commerce, Bureau of the Census, *Fifteenth Census of the United States, 1930: Agriculture: The Southern States*, II, Pt. 2.

65 purchase of farm properties by timber and mining companies and for <u>inclusion</u> in
66 national forests and parks.[5]
67   Farm productivity and income also changed. While farm production had been the
68 major (and usually the sole) source of income in 1880, by 1930 most mountain farms had
69 become part-time units of production, and the major source of income had shifted to
70 nonagricultural employment—mining, logging, textiles, and other forms of public work.[6]
71   Along with the decline of agriculture came subtle changes in demographic relation-
72 ships as well. Whereas mountain society in the 1880s had been characterized by a diffuse
73 pattern of open-country agricultural settlements located primarily in the fertile valleys
74 and plateaus, by the turn of the century the population had begun to shift into non-
75 agricultural areas and to concentrate around centers of industrial growth. Between 1900
76 and 1930, the urban population of the region increased fourfold and the rural nonfarm
77 population almost twofold, while the farm population itself increased by only 5 percent.[7]
78 A few of the <u>burgeoning</u> urban centers were destined to be temporary communities, such
79 as the big timber towns of Sunburst and Ravensford in the Great Smoky Mountains, but
80 most were permanent settlements that had a lasting impact upon mountain life. It is
81 important to point out, moreover, that the majority of these new industrial communities
82 were company towns. In fact, over six hundred company towns were constructed in the
83 southern mountains during this period, and in the coal fields they outnumbered indepen-
84 dent incorporated towns more than five to one.[8]
85   This rising urban population provided a base for the <u>emergence</u> of a more modern
86 political system in the mountains, one increasingly dominated by corporate interests and
87 business-minded politicians. As a result, there emerged in Appalachia a constricted
88 political system based upon an economic hierarchy—those who controlled the jobs also
89 controlled the political system, and those who controlled the political system used their
90 power to <u>exploit</u> the region's natural wealth for their own personal gain. This loss of local
91 political control naturally distressed many mountain people and <u>plunged</u> the region into
92 prolonged industrial violence and social <u>strife</u>.[9]
93   Behind this transition in political culture lay the integration of the region into the
94 national economy and the subordination of local interests to those of outside corporations.
95 Nowhere was this process more evident than in the concentration of large amounts of
96 mountain lands in the hands of absentee owners. For example, in that portion of western
97 North Carolina, which later became the Great Smoky Mountains National Park, over 75
98 percent of the land came under the control of thirteen corporations, and one timber

[5] U.S. Department of Agriculture, *Economic and Social Problems and Conditions of the Southern Appalachians,* Miscellaneous Publication no. 205 (Washington, D.C., 1935), 16; Lewis Cecil Gray, "Economic Conditions and Tendencies in the Southern Appalachians as Indicated by the Cooperative Survey," *Mountain Life and Work,* 9, no. 2 (July 1933), 9.

[6] U.S. Department of Agriculture, *Economic and Social Conditions,* 3, 16.

[7] Gray, "Economic Conditions in the Southern Appalachians," 8; U.S. Department of Agriculture, *Economic and Social Conditions,* 120–21.

[8] U.S. Congress, Senate, *Report of the United States Coal Commission,* Sen. Doc. 195, 68th Cong. 2nd sess. (Washington, D.C., 1925), Table 14, p. 1467; U.S. Department of Commerce, Bureau of the Census, *Thirteenth Census of the United States, 1910: Population,* II and III.

[9] See Gordon B. McKinney, "Industrialization and Violence in Appalachia in the 1890's," in Williamson, ed., *An Appalachian Symposium,* 131–44.

99 company alone owned over a third of the total acreage.[10] The situation was even worse in
100 the coal fields. According to the West Virginia State Board of Agriculture in 1900, outside
101 capitalists owned 90 percent of the coal in Mingo County, 90 percent of the coal in Wayne
102 County, and 60 percent of that in Boone and McDowell counties.[11] Today, absentee
103 corporations control more than half the total land area in the nine southernmost counties
104 of the Mountain State.[12]
105   The immediate effect of this <u>concentration</u> of landholding was to <u>dislodge</u> a large part
106 of the region's people from their ancestral homes. A few former landowners managed to
107 remain on the land as sharecroppers or tenant farmers, and occasionally a family
108 continued to live temporarily on the old homeplace, paying rent to absentee landlords.[13]
109 But a great number of displaced mountaineers migrated to the mill villages and mining
110 towns, where they joined the ever-growing <u>ranks</u> of the new industrial working class. In
111 the Cumberland Plateau, less than a third of those employed in 1930 remained in
112 agriculture. The rest had moved to the mines or into service-related jobs.[14] Uprooted
113 from their traditional way of life, some individuals were unable to reestablish permanent
114 community ties, and they became wanderers drifting from mill to mill, from company
115 house to company house, in search of higher pay or better living conditions. Most
116 dreamed initially of returning to the land after a few years of public work, but the rising
117 land values that accompanied industrial development soon pushed land ownership
118 beyond the reach of the average miner or millhand.
119   Caught up in the social complex of the new industrial communities, many moun-
120 taineers found themselves unable to escape their condition of powerlessness and depen-
121 dency. By coming to a coal-mining town, the miner had exchanged the independence and
122 somewhat precarious self-sufficiency of the family farm for subordination to the coal
123 company and dependence upon a wage income. He lived in a company house, he worked
124 in the company mine, and he purchased his groceries and other commodities from the
125 company store. He sent his children to the company school and patronized the company
126 doctor and the company church. The company deducted rent and school, medical, and
127 other fees from his monthly wage, and, under the prevailing system of scrip, he
128 occasionally ended the month without a cash income. He had no voice in community
129 affairs or working conditions, and he was dependent upon the <u>benevolence</u> of the
130 employer to maintain his rate of pay.
131   By 1930, most mountaineers, whether they remained on the farm or migrated to the
132 mill villages, timber towns, or coal camps, had become socially integrated within the new
133 industrial system and economically dependent upon it as well. To say the least, this

[10] Map, *North Carolina Portion of the Great Smoky Mountains National Park, Showing Individual Ownership*, Western Carolina Univ., University Archives, Hunter Library.

[11] West Virginia, State Board of Agriculture, *Fifth Biennial Report of the West Virginia State Board of Agriculture for the Years 1899 and 1900* (Charleston, W.Va., 1900), 371.

[12] Tom D. Miller, "Absentees Dominate Land Ownership," in *Who Owns West Virginia?*, reprinted from the *Herald Adviser* and the *Herald-Dispatch* (Huntington, W.Va., 1974), 1–3.

[13] James Lane Allen, "Mountain Passes of the Cumberlands," *Harper's Magazine* 81 (Sept. 1890), 575; Herbert Francis Sherwood, "Our New Racial Drama: Southern Mountaineers in the Textile Industry," *North American Review* 216 (Oct. 1922), 494; John C. Campbell, *The Southern Highlander and His Homeland* (Lexington, Ky, 1969) 87, 314.

[14] U.S. Department of Agriculture, *Economic and Social Conditions*, 3.

134 dependence was not on their own terms—that is to say, it was a product not of mountain
135 culture but of the same political and economic forces that were shaping the rest of the
136 nation and the western world. The rise of industrial capitalism brought to Appalachia a
137 period of rapid growth and social change which those who hold to the static image have
138 chosen to ignore. The brief prosperity brought on by the bonanza of modernization
139 broadened the mountaineer's economic horizon. It aroused aspirations, envies, and
140 hopes. But the industrial wonders of the age promised more than they in fact delivered,
141 for the profits taken from the rich natural resources of the region flowed out of the
142 mountains, with little benefit to the mountain people themselves. For a relative handful of
143 owners and managers, the new order yielded riches unimaginable a few decades before;
144 for thousands of mountaineers, it brought a life of struggle, hardship, and despair.
145 Considered from this perspective, the persistent poverty of Appalachia has not resulted
146 from the lack of modernization. Rather, it has come from the particular kind of
147 modernization that unfolded in the years from 1880 to 1930.

Reading for Full Comprehension

1. T/F   The author would agree that Appalachia is backward.

2. What does the word "they" on line 13 refer to?

3. What metaphor does the word "metaphor" on line 22 refer to?

4. On line 32, the author mentions "this revival of interest." The use of the
    word "this" indicates that specific examples of the "revival of interest" can
    be found in preceding lines. What are some specific examples of "this
    revival of interest" mentioned in the lines before line 32?

5. What does "notion" in line 3 refer to?

6. What is the "static image" the author refers to on line 26?

7. What are the "forces" referred to on line 47?

8. What does "it" on line 47 refer to?

9. Give specific examples of "this transformation" on line 56.

10. What does the subject noun clause "what had been in 1860 only the quiet
    backcountry of the Old South" refer to?

11. In lines 38–41, the author compares history to _____
    _____. What specific words does he use to create this meta-
    phor?

12. Give specific examples of "this concentration of landholding" mentioned
    in the lines preceding line 105.

13. T/F   The idea that Appalachia is "different" is a recent one.

14. T/F   The idea of Appalachia is the idea Americans had of the American
    past.

15. How do Americans measure progress? Do Americans see Appalachia as a progressive region?

    How does the author define modernization?

16. Give examples of how companies controlled the lives of people who lived in company towns.

    What effect did changes in land ownership have upon the Appalachian people?

17. How and why did the population of Appalachia move in the period from 1880 to 1930?

    What effect did the growth of cities have upon Appalachian political systems?

18. Is the contemporary view of Appalachia different from the traditional one?

19. How do Americans explain the social problems of Appalachia? How should Americans explain the problems according to the author?

20. Which of the following agricultural changes took place in the period from 1880 to 1930? Indicate the lines on which you found the answers.
    a. There were more farms. (Y/N) _____.
    b. Farm sizes increased. (Y/N) _____.
    c. There were more full-time farmers. (Y/N) _____.

21. List the negative effects of industrial capitalism on the people of Appalachia.

22. Has Appalachia, as many Americans believe, been unaffected by modernization? Explain your answer.

23. Summarize this reading selection in 75 to 100 words.

READING #2

Prereading

Directions: These are some words that you will need to understand before reading the passage.

back-to-the-land movement (noun phrase): a movement to return people to farms and a rural lifestyle.

the Nixon Administration (noun phrase): the administration of United States President Richard M. Nixon from 1968 to 1974.

over the long pull (adv.): over a long, difficult time.

Vocabulary in Context

Directions: Read the following passage without using your dictionary. As you read the passage, try to guess the meaning of the following words, all of which are underlined in the passage. Write your guesses in the appropriate column and look up the words in an English-English dictionary to check your guesses. Then reread the passage, using your dictionary, and do the exercises at the end of the passage.

Words	My Guess	Dictionary Definition
tackled		
migration		
shifting		
prosperity		
lags		
commute		
generated		

Words	My Guess	Dictionary Definition
ruled out		
labor sheds		
accelerate		
appropriates		

What are two phrases in the sentence that goes from line 73 to 76 that mean the same as "labor sheds"?

PROGRESS IN APPALACHIA: A MODEL FOR FEDERAL AID?

From: U.S. News & World Report, March 23, 1970, pp. 79–80.

1   The Nixon Administration, in its search for a new policy to guide the growth of
2   America, is looking at an area that a decade ago was regarded as a symbol of
3   backwardness—Appalachia.
4   Officials believe the regional development program that began there in 1965 is
5   working. In addition, the special problems of Appalachia are being tackled in a way that
6   seems to fit the President's notion of how the federal government and the states should
7   work together.
8   **Threefold problem.** A decade ago, an average of 220,000 persons per year were
9   leaving Appalachia. Average income was far below the national level. Unemployment was
10 nearly double that for the nation as a whole.
11   The number of people leaving the area has dropped to about one-third the level of
12 the 1950s. In another ten years, the movement out of Appalachia is expected to be no
13 problem.
14   The character of the migration has changed, too. Once it was primarily poor people
15 shifting to the cities of the Midwest and Northeast. Now, much of the movement is into

16 nearby areas of the South, such as the Carolina Piedmont or Atlanta, or into urban sections
17 of Appalachia itself.
18   On the basis of two important measures of prosperity—average income and the rate
19 of unemployment—this region has actually shown more rapid improvement during the
20 last few years than the rest of the nation. Appalachia still lags behind in both respects, but it
21 is catching up, officials insist.
22   The Appalachian Regional Commission was created in 1965 with a pipeline straight
23 into the White House through a federal co-chairman named by the President. Its area of
24 concern is all of West Virginia and parts of New York, Pennsylvania, Ohio, Maryland,
25 Kentucky, Virginia, Tennessee, North and South Carolina, Alabama, Georgia, and
26 Mississippi.
27   Governors of all these states are Commission members. Their goal is to speed up
28 economic development and reduce poverty.
29   Most of Appalachia is mountainous. There is little good farmland. Even homesites
30 are scarce in some rugged areas. Coal mining, still an important industry, accounts for
31 only about 3 percent of the jobs in the region.
32   In its first five years, the ARC has spent slightly more than a billion dollars of federal
33 money. The first big program was a network of roads designed to open up isolated areas.
34 Originally, 2,700 miles were planned. Rising costs cut this back by about one-third to
35 1,752. So far:
36   · 248 miles of roads have been completed.
37   · 422 miles are still under construction.
38   · 1,082 miles are being engineered or have right-of-way work under way.
39   One early result of the road-building has been to make it possible to commute from
40 Hazard, Ky., a mountain community with an excess labor supply, to Lexington, where jobs
41 are available. Before 1968, the trip took $3^{1}/_{2}$ hours. Now, it takes $1^{1}/_{2}$ hours.
42   In trying to provide a broader base for future growth, these projects either have been
43 finished or are being built:
44   · 238 vocational schools.
45   · 120 higher-education facilities, mostly community colleges.
46   · 193 health units, mostly hospitals.
47   · 72 libraries.
48   · 43 airports.
49   · 160 water-pollution programs.
50   · 55 mine-rehabilitation projects.
51   The Commission has a regional housing program that in a year and a half has
52 generated construction of 4,848 units. This is roughly twelve times as many federally
53 subsidized housing units as had been built in the period 1965–68, officials say.
54   In Appalachia, the emphasis is on urban but not metropolitan growth—and also on
55 making it easier for people to live in the country and work in the city.
56   Ninety percent of the population increase for the nation as a whole from 1960 to 1966
57 came in metropolitan counties—around the largest cities. In Appalachia, about 40 percent
58 of the expansion in this period came in much smaller urban counties—where the
59 population was 10,000 to 50,000.

60 ARC planners long ago <u>ruled out</u> any back-to-the-land movement or effort merely to
61 bring in new factories. For one thing, Appalachia already has a greater proportion of its
62 employment in manufacturing than the U.S. as a whole.

63 For another, experts say, the big problem is a lack of urban centers large enough to
64 provide a service base for industry already there. Most new jobs opening up today are in
65 service industries—stores, laundries, restaurants.

66 **Role of the cities.** Urbanization, says ARC Executive Director Ralph Widner, is the
67 process through which services of all sorts are delivered to people. These industries help
68 recirculate payrolls and multiply the economic benefits, he explains.

69 "If we refuse to recognize the essential role which urbanization must play in rural
70 development," Mr. Widner says, "we will have local economies that 'leak' local industrial
71 and agricultural-payroll dollars [that leave the community]—leaks that over the long pull
72 can sink any economies."

73 Also, he adds: "The Commission recognized that the nation has become essentially a
74 network of <u>labor sheds</u> or service areas with urban complexes at their core, and that these
75 areas are presently the basic functional economic units in the national economy and in
76 Appalachia and should be the basic planning units for any regional development efforts."

77 Thus, the goal in Appalachia is to make these labor sheds as efficient as possible, with
78 jobs, health services, education, and the like readily accessible to all who live in the area.

79 Appalachia is divided into 60 local planning and development districts. They are
80 made up of several counties each, with one or more existing or planned areas of potential
81 growth in each district. There are 22 regional centers, which are larger communities that
82 serve several districts; 78 primary centers, where significant expansion is expected and
83 major investments are intended; and 88 secondary centers, where only enough educa-
84 tional and health facilities will be provided to take care of nearby rural areas.

85 **Community planning.** Each district works out its own plan for economic develop-
86 ment. Usually, local officials seek to <u>accelerate</u> trends already under way. For example,
87 when several sections of the interstate highway system passed close by the Scranton-
88 Wilkes-Barre area of Pennsylvania, a new function developed for these communities as a
89 distribution center for the region around New York City, 100 miles away. ARC then was
90 called on to help build industrial parks and other facilities needed to expand this new role.

91 In eastern Kentucky, an urban service area is evolving around three small towns—
92 Pikeville, Prestonsburg, and Paintsville—to serve a surrounding population of 300,000
93 persons. Most of the growth centers in Appalachia are planned in this fashion around
94 existing towns or clusters of towns.

95 However, in some districts there is no community large enough for a growth nucleus,
96 though there still is a relatively thick rural population. Here new towns are being created.

97 Examples of these new communities are Midland, Ky., on Interstate 64 near More-
98 head; Lucasville, Ohio, a new town near Portsmouth; and Fairdale, a new town site near
99 Beckley, W.Va.

100 **Allocation of funds.** Not only is the planning a bit different in Appalachia, but the
101 way the money is spent is different, too.

102 Congress <u>appropriates</u> money to the ARC for broad uses—highways, education,
103 health, and so on.

104 The Commission can shift some of this money from one purpose to another, if
105 requirements should change. The states, too, have some leeway to switch funds to fit the
106 needs of their overall plans.

107 Local and state planners work closely together in deciding on community projects.
108 They determine what portion the community can pay, how much is needed from the
109 ARC, and where to go for other funds.

110 Small towns often have fared badly in seeking federal aid because a good deal of
111 know-how is necessary to keep track of the many programs and their complex require-
112 ments. Through use of multicounty districts working with state experts, a poor commu-
113 nity in Appalachia can gain some of the resources of a larger, more prosperous city in
114 bidding for additional federal funds.

115 Five other regional commissions have been established under the Economic Develop-
116 ment Act and operate under the Department of Commerce.

117 **"Partnership."** How do the governors like the program? Says Governor Arch A.
118 Moore of West Virginia:

119 "Never before has there been a federal-state partnership quite like the one in this Act,
120 and it works.

121 "Every single one of the governors of the Appalachian states—and we cover the whole
122 range of the political spectrum—likes this program."

123 Administration planners see this as a possible working model of Mr. Nixon's "new
124 federalism." State and local officials plan and make decisions together, with emphasis on
125 building up moderate-size cities around existing small towns, plus some new towns to take
126 pressures off metropolitan areas, and private economic growth is heavily stressed instead
127 of continued federal aid.

Reading for Full Comprehension

1. What were the three major problems in Appalachia ten years ago?

2. Combine the facts in the sentence beginning, "A decade ago . . ." (line 8) and "the number of people . . ." (line 11) to calculate the number of people who left Appalachia in 1970.

3. What does the author predict about emigration in the year 1980?

4. Where did most of the people who left in 1960 go? Where did most of the people who left in 1970 go? Is this a positive or negative change? Why?

5. What two economic measures had shown improvement at the time this article was written?

6. Which state is entirely part of Appalachia?

7. When was the ARC formed? Why was it formed?

8. What percentage of jobs does coal mining supply?

9. Why is road building so important in Appalachia?

10. If all completed, semicompleted, or engineered roads are counted, how many miles will be built?

11. How many educational complexes are or will be built?

12. How many federally subsidized homes were built between 1965–68? Which statistics could you use to calculate this number?

13. What is the difference between a metropolitan county (line 57) and a smaller urban county (line 58)?

14. Why doesn't Appalachia need new factories to be developed there?

15. According to Ralph Widner, how will urbanization help Appalachia? Without urbanization, what happens to the money local people earn?

16. In lines 70 to 72, using the words "leak" and "sink," Ralph Widner compares the economy of Appalachia to a _____.

17. What are the growth areas planned for Appalachia?

18. How has a road made an economic difference in the Scranton-Wilkes-Barre area?

19. Where does the ARC get its money?

20. T/F Individual projects sponsored by the ARC are totally funded by the ARC.

21. One way an author can give us information indirectly is by inference. For example, a writer could say, "She's different from her husband. She's one of the most outgoing people I've ever known."

    In this way, the reader knows two points: She is outgoing and her husband is not outgoing. On line 101 the author mentions that "the way money is spent [in Appalachia] is different, too." On line 115 he mentions there are five other regional commissions. Now, read lines 102 to 106 and list some ways in which the money is probably spent by the other regional commissions.

22. What do the members of the ARC think about this commission?

23. What are some of the characteristics of the "new federalism" mentioned on lines 123–124?

24. After reading this article are you optimistic about the ARC and the economic future of Appalachia? Why or why not?

25. Summarize this reading selection in 75 to 100 words.

READING #3

Prereading

Directions: These are some of the words that you will need to understand before reading the passage.

disability payments (compound noun): government-funded payments made to workers who have been injured or made ill by their jobs.

food stamps (compound noun): government-provided coupons that enable needy people to obtain free or low-cost food.

Great Society (noun phrase): a term used to refer to the many social welfare programs begun in the 1960s during the administration of President Lyndon Johnson.

high tech (abbreviation): high technology.

light years (compound noun): thousands of miles.

Lyndon Johnson (proper noun): a president of the United States during the 1960s.

out of favor with (adj.) disliked; unpopular.

Vocabulary in Context

Directions: Read the following passage without using your dictionary. As you read the passage, try to guess the meaning of the following words, all of which are underlined in the passage. Write your guesses in the appropriate column and look up the words in an English-English dictionary to check your guesses. Then reread the passage, using your dictionary, and do the exercises at the end of the passage.

Words	My Guess	Dictionary Definition
perched		
balked		

Words	My Guess	Dictionary Definition
exodus		
quips		
clamoring		
to tackle		
devastating		
mortgages		

APPALACHIA: A LAND WITH TWO FACES

by S. Huntley

From: U.S. News & World Report, August 18, 1986, pp. 18–19.

Hazard, Ky.

1   All that separates the lives of Junie Handshoe and Ken James is about sixty miles and
2 several light-years.
3   Handshoe, widow of a coal miner, is one of Appalachia's ever-present poor. Home is a
4 three-room shack without running water, <u>perched</u> on the side of a deep valley formed by a
5 branch of Troublesome Creek in eastern Kentucky. The necessities of life come by way of
6 $250 a month in Social Security and disability payments plus food stamps. "We don't have
7 no easy time here," says Handshoe, 64. "I don't like this place, but it don't cost nothing, so I
8 guess I'll be here till I die."

⁹ An hour's drive down the Daniel Boone Parkway is London and Ken James, 47, one
¹⁰ of Appalachia's success stories. The steady click-clicking produced by scores of women
¹¹ pounding the keyboards of video display terminals at Appalachian Computer Services is
¹² the realization of his vision of "bringing high tech to the hills." The company that James
¹³ heads converts clients' documents into electronic files and expects to have sales of $30
¹⁴ million this year—more than forty times higher than it had ten years ago.

¹⁵ The two faces of Appalachia—one poor, one prosperous—persist after two decades
¹⁶ of federal spending totaling $5 billion in efforts to penetrate the geographic, economic,
¹⁷ and cultural isolation of a mountain region that spans thirteen states from New York to
¹⁸ Mississippi. Born in Lyndon Johnson's Great Society, the Appalachian Regional Commis-
¹⁹ sion (ARC) is out of favor with the administration of Ronald Reagan, which tried to kill it.
²⁰ Congress balked, however, and is likely to recommend funding of $105 million for 1987,
²¹ less than a third of the budget under Jimmy Carter.

²² "Until the ARC is dead, we're not going to admit that it can die," declares Percy Elkins,
²³ executive director of the Kentucky River Area Development District, based at Hazard.

²⁴ The diminished ARC role comes at a time when the mountain people face an
²⁵ economic crisis that, for some, rivals that of the Depression, says Ronald Eller, director of
²⁶ the Appalachian Center at the University of Kentucky. The region has been sliding
²⁷ downhill since 1980 because of a falloff in coal prices amid the oil glut, mine mechaniza-
²⁸ tion that has cost jobs, a decline in basic industries, and the lingering aftershock of the
²⁹ 1981–82 recession.

³⁰ **The score card**

³¹ The eight-county Kentucky River district has received $28.7 million in ARC funds for
³² education, health, water, and sewage projects and millions more for highway improve-
³³ ments. Results from this twenty-one-year investment, says Elkins, reflect both the success
³⁴ of federal intervention and the magnitude of the task still to be done—

³⁵ · The district's unemployment rate is down from a high of 28 percent in 1965 to 17
³⁶ percent, still more than twice the national average. In some counties, the rate approaches
³⁷ 35 or 40 percent.

³⁸ · The poverty level fell from 48 percent in 1970 to an estimated 31 percent last year,
³⁹ compared with the U.S. average of 14.4 percent in 1984.

⁴⁰ · An exodus of people in the 1950s and '60s was reversed for a while, and the district's
⁴¹ population in the last two decades jumped by 39,000 to 135,000, but that's still 30,000
⁴² fewer than in 1950. Now the young are leaving again.

⁴³ · The mountains still have a 50 percent school-dropout rate, and a third of the people are
⁴⁴ functionally illiterate.

⁴⁵ · As much as 50 percent of the water in southeastern Kentucky is contaminated from strip-
⁴⁶ mine runoff, poor land use, and inadequate solid-waste disposal.

⁴⁷ Crucial to economic development over the past twenty years, everyone in the hills will
⁴⁸ tell you, are roads, which have absorbed nearly two-thirds of the federal funds. The ARC
⁴⁹ assumed about 70 percent of the $100.9 million cost of some eighty miles of State Highway
⁵⁰ 15 linking the Kentucky River district to major east-west and north-south routes.

⁵¹ Completion of the road in the 1970s coincided with the energy crunch, enabling
⁵² miners to truck coal to the Ohio River and to utilities in the Midwest. The boom helped
⁵³ generate 17,000 jobs, some of which have been lost with the drop in coal prices. "You could
⁵⁴ sell anything that was half black," quips Ann Medaris of Hazard.

⁵⁵ Rural areas of Appalachia are <u>clamoring</u> for still more roads. Thus far, the ARC has
⁵⁶ completed 2,000 miles of the 3,000 miles it planned to build, but some doubt the rest will
⁵⁷ be done anytime soon. Reason: Soaring costs of mountain roads. The bill was $27 million
⁵⁸ for just 2.2 miles of the Highway 15 bypass at Hazard. The national average for rural
⁵⁹ highways yet to be completed is $1.8 million per mile.

⁶⁰ Blasting through the mountains to construct the roads left tons of earth and rock with
⁶¹ which to fill hollows and make level building sites. Hazard has a public park, swimming
⁶² pool, subsidized housing project, and a television station—all built on such acreage. In
⁶³ nearby Jackson, the highway work chopped off a loop in the Kentucky River that had
⁶⁴ caused frequent flooding. Left in its place are a small lake and 400 acres of dry, flat land
⁶⁵ that has become the site of an industrial park, medical clinic, shops, and businesses
⁶⁶ employing 500 people.

⁶⁷ Besides more and better roads, backers of the ARC say, an extended federal
⁶⁸ commitment is necessary <u>to tackle</u> such high-priority needs as water, garbage collections,
⁶⁹ and housing.

⁷⁰ **Creatures in the water tap**

⁷¹ Many families living outside towns along the Kentucky River pipe water to their
⁷² homes in the hollows from abandoned mines in the mountains.

⁷³ Some find the water, with a sharp mineral taste, refreshing, but Kathy Smith, 34, of
⁷⁴ Tribbey was thankful when her mobile home was hooked up to a city line. "When you
⁷⁵ boiled that mine water, an awful yellow skim would come to the top," she says. "Sometimes
⁷⁶ water dogs [salamanders] would clog up in the pipe."

⁷⁷ Only two of the district's eight counties have enforced solid-waste collection. "Too
⁷⁸ many people just throw their garbage on someone's property, in a creek, along a road,"
⁷⁹ says one official. Adds Jim Brashear, a native of Letcher County: "Don't come to the
⁸⁰ mountains in the fall or winter unless you want to be depressed. After the leaves are gone,
⁸¹ you can see garbage and litter all over the hillsides."

⁸² Lynn Luallen, executive director of the Kentucky Housing Corporation, says eastern
⁸³ Kentucky needs 5,000 units of new housing a year. Loss of federal funds could prove
⁸⁴ <u>devastating</u> to the Kentucky Mountain Housing Development Corporation in Manches-
⁸⁵ ter. The nonprofit group builds three-bedroom homes priced down to $16,000 and
⁸⁶ finances them for low-income families through <u>mortgages</u> with an effective interest rate of
⁸⁷ 1 percent.

⁸⁸ Buying a subsidized house from Kentucky Mountain was the only way Bessie Melton,
⁸⁹ 61, could afford a new home. She and her late husband had lived in a leaky trailer with
⁹⁰ floors that threatened to give way. While emphasizing that she has never taken food
⁹¹ stamps or welfare, the bespectacled grandmother flashes a ready smile, gestures at her
⁹² well-kept ranch house and says, "It tickles me to brag on it."

⁹³ Backers of the government programs acknowledge that federal spending has not
⁹⁴ transformed the Kentucky River area from a one-industry economy. Coal is still king,
⁹⁵ ruling lives of rich and poor alike. One eastern Kentucky mine executive paid homage to
⁹⁶ the mineral that made him a fortune by erecting a block of it as a wall in the den of his
⁹⁷ home. Appalachian coal prices have dropped by more than a third from $36 a ton in 1979.
⁹⁸ A third of the unemployment-insurance payments in Hazard go to laid-off coal miners.

99   The betting here is that the nation's fears about acid rain eventually will spell bigger
100 sales for the low-sulfur coal mined in the area. Yet mechanization is replacing workers,
101 and one study forecasts eastern Kentucky will lose 4,500 mining jobs by 1995.

102   Junie Handshoe's life mirrors some of the region's problems. While she talked with
103 visitors on a recent summer day, her 19-year-old daughter Teresa did laundry in an old
104 washer on the open front porch while Teresa's 13-month-old son, Arthur Lee, watched
105 from the doorway.

106   Teenagers account for 1 in every 5 pregnancies in Kentucky, and the state in 1983
107 had the highest rate of births to white teenagers in the country. Handshoe has a 23-year-
108 old daughter with seven children. "Standing together, they look like a set of steps going
109 up," she says.

110   Women in these parts have so many children so early that, by the time they are in their
111 thirties, many seek sterilization. By one count, Hazard's hospital in June had a waiting list
112 of 135 women seeking tubular ligation.

113   Children born into mountain poverty find it tough to escape. Gordon Slone, 11, lives
114 on welfare and food stamps with his mother, Bethel Lee Slone, 34, and six siblings. Their
115 home is a 12-by-24-foot, two-room house painted yellow and topped with a corrugated tin
116 roof, near Caney Creek in Knott County. Standing in the doorway keeping an eye on a TV
117 set, a shirtless, towheaded Gordon expresses an interest in math but then blurts out, "I
118 hate school. When I get to the eighth grade, I'm going to quit."

119   His mother glances over her children and remarks, "Sure, I'd like for them to grow up
120 to be doctors and lawyers." Then, without much conviction, she adds, "I just hope for the
121 best."

122   Such acceptance of life as it is is not uncommon. "I was born a poor boy," says Justin
123 White, 51, who lives with his ailing wife and four sons in a three-bedroom house with
124 indoor plumbing at the end of a winding, rutted dirt road in Ogden Hollow. "I've never
125 lived better."

126 **"The reality"**

127   Some worry that government welfare only reinforces the cycle of poverty. "Our
128 people are too passive," complains a Hazard resident. "They've been cared for too long.
129 They need to be pushed out of the nest."

130   The Appalachian Center's Ronald Eller warns against quick judgments: "What seems
131 fatalistic frequently is actually an acceptance of powerlessness. The reality is, given the
132 opportunity to work, mountain people will work."

133   However resistant poverty remains to Washington's solutions, Judge Executive
134 Homer Sawyer of Knott County delivers the verdict on government aid that is heard
135 everywhere around here: "People are climbing out of poverty, and we've got a growing
136 number of moderate-to-average-income families. Things are 100 percent better than
137 twenty years ago."

Reading for Full Comprehension

1. Compare the information in the two reports. How old was the ARC at the time of the first report? The second report?

2. How much money had been spent by the ARC at the time of the first report? At the time of the second report?

3. How many miles of road did the ARC plan to build at the time of the first report? At the time of the second report?

4. How many miles were built or were in the process of being built at the time of the first report? At the time of the second report?

5. List an influence that that may cause the sales of coal to rise.

   List influences that have caused, or may cause the prices of coal to fall.

6. List two major reasons why coal miners are out of work.

7. Consider the predictions the author of the first article made about the emigration rate from Appalachia in 1970. Has his prediction, based on the example of the Kentucky River district, proven to be correct?

8. In the sixth paragraph the author uses the words "sliding downhill," "fall off," and "decline." By choosing these words, what is he saying about the general state of the Appalachian economy?

9. In the first sentence, what is the author saying about the differences that exist in Appalachia?

10. One of the techniques that authors can use in writing a report is to depersonalize and personalize the facts they present. A depersonalized report usually shows "the big picture" and rarely mentions how the facts influence individuals. A personalized report brings a small focus to the information and often shows how the facts influence individuals.

    Which of these two reports is more personalized?

    What makes the report more personal?

    Which is more interesting to read?

    Which one makes you feel more optimistic?

11. What are some ways better roads have helped Appalachia?

12. What are three problems Appalachia still faces?

13. How much is Appalachian coal per ton?

14. What might be one reason for the high school dropout rate?

15. T/F   Under President Carter the ARC's budget was $315 million.

16. Summarize this reading selection in 75 to 100 words.

THE MOVIE: COAL MINER'S DAUGHTER

Photofest

A. How would you describe these people?

B. Do they seem happy to you?

About the Movie

This movie begins in Butcher Holler, a poor coal-mining town in the Appalachian Mountains of Kentucky. Thirteen-year-old Loretta Webb, the child of a coal miner, meets Doolittle Lynn, a local boy who had just returned from fighting in World War II. Soon, Loretta and "Doo" (his friends call him Mooney) realize they are in love and get married.

Cultural Points about the Movie

The Grand Ole Opry is the name of a music hall and a radio show in Nashville, Tennessee. It is considered an important place for country music singers to perform. A popular country music radio show is broadcast every week from the Opry.

Movie Vocabulary

Directions: These are some of the words that you will need to understand before seeing the movie. Look them up in your dictionary, or ask an American friend for the definitions. Write the letter of the correct definition in front of each word.

_____ **ain't:**
_____ **hillbilly** (compound noun):
_____ **honky-tonk** (noun/verb):
_____ **moonshine** (noun):
_____ **picker** (noun):

a.   A bar where country music is played; to go to such a bar.

b.   A nonstandard form of the English negative. It can be used to replace be + negative in the present tenses and have + negative in the present perfect tenses.
Example: I ain't happy with this. He ain't had any money for a long time.

c.   A negative way of referring to a person from Appalachia. It means a dull, slow, ignorant person.

d.   a guitar player.

e.   An illegal, extremely strong whiskey made in Appalachia. It is often just called "shine."

As You Watch the Movie

Directions: Read the following questions. Keep them in mind while you watch the movie. After the movie, discuss your answers to these questions with a small group of your classmates.

This is the story of a woman who left Appalachia and then returned. As you watch the movie, consider the different social problems that impact the lives of Loretta and her family. What problems does the movie show? How do Loretta and her family deal with them?

It is also the story of one woman's professional success. What forces helped her earn this success? How did she change as her professional career succeeded?

Postmovie Discussion Questions

1. Describe some of the ways the director shows the poverty of Appalachia.

2. What are some of the social problems that are shown in the movie?

3. What doesn't Loretta know about when she gets married?

4. What are Loretta's family like? What are their reactions to her marriage and pregnancy?

5. How does "Doo" feel about Appalachia? What kind of action does he take because of his feelings?

6. What are Loretta's initial feelings about performing? What are Doo's feelings?

7. At what point in the movie do Doo's and Loretta's feelings change? How does the director show this change in feeling?

8. How do Loretta's songs reflect the experiences of her life?

9. Why did Loretta suffer her nervous breakdown?

Movie Review #1

Prereading

*Directions: These are some words that you will need to understand before reading
            the passage.*

cracker-barrel wit (compound noun): simple, country wit and intelligence.

to hit it big (verbal idiom): to be successful.

Vocabulary in Context

*Directions: Read the following passage without using your dictionary. As you read
            the passage, try to guess the meaning of the following words, all of which
            have been underlined in the passage. Write your guesses in the appropri-
            ate column and look up the words in an English-English dictionary to
            check your guesses. Then reread the passage, using your dictionary, and
            do the exercises at the end of the passage.*

Words	My Guess	Dictionary Definition
homestead		
protagonist		
conveyed		
delineated		

STARSTRUCK
Review of Coal Miner's Daughter

From: *Time*, March 10, 1980. Copyright © 1980, Time, Inc. Reprinted by permission

1   For about half its length, this film biography of country singer Loretta Lynn outdoes
2 even "The Buddy Holly Story" and "The Rose" in the show-biz-saga sweepstakes. Care
3 and intelligence are everywhere in evidence. British director Michael Apted ("Agatha")
4 captures both the poverty and pride of the young Loretta's Appalachian homestead
5 without resorting to Hollywood sentimentality or glamorization. Tom Rickman's script
6 uses intimate, telling details as it enthusiastically describes the heroine's gradual transfor-
7 mation from thirteen-year-old hillbilly bride to Nashville superstar. The cast, especially
8 Sissy Spacek as Lynn—the best role of her career—is always winning.
9   So what goes wrong? As it sadly turns out, "Coal Miner's Daughter" is not entirely
10 immune to the tired conventions of backstage movie melodramas. No sooner does Lynn
11 start to hit it big than the film ineluctably slips into the usual "Star Is Born" clichés.
12 Suddenly, and with only the slightest motivation, the protagonist is afflicted by marital
13 conflict, pill addiction, desperate loneliness, and a nervous collapse. True, these tragedies
14 happened in life, but in the movie they seem phony: Lynn's later personal traumas are not
15 so much dramatized as displayed like flash cards for predictable audience response. As the
16 screenplay loses its energy, so does most everything else. Apted's direction takes on the
17 facile, rushed quality of his 1975 film about the rise of a rock star, "Stardust". Spacek's big
18 scene, her onstage breakdown, is so imprecisely drawn that she has no chance to duplicate
19 the pathos Ronee Blakley brought to a fictive version of the same incident in "Nashville."
20   Deflating as these anticlimaxes are, they still do not alter the achievement of what has
21 gone before. The early scenes, which unfold in the green hills and gaslit haunts of a dusky
22 rural mining town, are full of flavor and native humor. When the pallid, naive Loretta
23 marries an Army veteran of 19 (Tommy Lee Jones) and moves with him to Washington
24 state to raise a family, the couple's first ignorant encounters with sex and the outside world
25 are conveyed with tender humor rather than condescension. When Loretta gets her first
26 guitar and starts to pick and sing, the audience has no choice but to root for her. Her early
27 successes—in local honky-tonks, on radio, and at the Grand Ole Opry—are thrilling
28 because the movie has so carefully delineated just how hard she has worked and how far
29 she has come to realize her show-biz fantasy.
30   Spacek not only ages and sings convincingly, but she gives her character a spine of
31 strong emotion, of pure innocence, and instinctive cracker-barrel wit. Inside the shy and
32 often childish teenage girl there is always a glimmer of the powerhouse woman she would
33 become. The craggy-faced Jones makes the most of a role that fully capitalizes on both his
34 redneck swagger and salty charm. The supporting cast is also first-rate. Rock drummer
35 Levon Helm (formerly of the Band) brings flinty dignity to the role of Loretta's laconic but
36 loving father, and Beverly D'Angelo (who played Sheila in "Hair") has a riotous time

37 impersonating country singer Patsy Cline. Like Loretta Lynn's music, the characters in
38 "Coal Miner's Daughter" stay in the mind long after the drama that contains them runs
39 out.

Reading for Full Comprehension

1. Consider the compound noun "show-biz-saga sweepstakes" on line 2. Look up the words "saga" and "sweepstakes." To read a compound noun like this, start with the last noun and connect it to the second-to-last noun with a preposition. "Of," "for," and "about" are good prepositions to try. For example, "A sweepstakes of sagas about show biz" is one way to read this compound noun. Using definitions to replace those words you will probably come up with something like "a competition of long stories about the entertainment industry." Given this reading, what movies are in the competition? Which is the best? What does it indicate about the stories of the movies on line 2?

2. How much of this movie does the author like?

3. At what point in the movie does the author believe the movie begins to lose its quality?

4. What particular scenes did the author most enjoy? List them. Explain his specific reasons for liking them.

5. The author mentions four actors. List them. Underline his comments about each actor. What is his opinion of each actor?

6. What is the reviewer's reason for saying that the movie uses "Star Is Born" clichés?

7. Which breakdown scene was better, according to the author, the one in "Coal Miner's Daughter" or the one in "Nashville"?

8. List all the movies that the director has directed.

9. What was Levon Helm's job before he became an actor?

10. Overall, would you say the author enjoyed this movie or not? Explain your answers.

11. Summarize this reading selection in 75 to 100 words.

MOVIE REVIEW #2

Prereading

Directions: These are some words that you will need to understand before reading the passage. After you have studied these words, read the passage twice without consulting a dictionary.

a ticket to (noun phrase): an opportunity, a chance for.

at the top of the heap (prep. phrase): in the leading position.

ditto (noun): the same.

in store for (prep. phrase): will have.

on-target (adj.): correct.

rags to riches (noun phrase): from poverty to wealth.

short shrift (noun phrase): too little attention.

sudsy (adj.): melodramatic, as in a soap opera.

to pull punches (verbal idiom): to give an unexpected shock.

to take a liking to (verbal idiom): to begin to like someone or something.

to hit the road (verbal idiom): to leave, to move on.

Vocabulary in Context

Directions: Read the following passage without using your dictionary. As you read the passage, try to guess the meaning of the following words, all of which have been underlined in the passage. Write your guesses in the appropriate column and look up the words in an English-English dictionary to check your guesses. Then reread the passage, using your dictionary, and do the exercises at the end of the passage.

Words   My Guess   Dictionary Definition

shoulders

siblings

Words	My Guess	Dictionary Definition
brood		
crimp		
ground		
penned		
drawback		
sagging		
ornery		
nuances		

COAL MINER'S DAUGHTER
Sissy Spacek captures the essence of Loretta Lynn.
Good outlook beyond country fans.

From: Berg, "Coal Miner's Daughter," *Variety,* February 20, 1980.

1   "Coal Miner's Daughter" is a thoughtful, endearing film charting the life of singer
2 Loretta Lynn from the depths of poverty in rural Kentucky to her eventual rise to the title
3 of "queen of country music." Thanks in large part to superb performances by Sissy Spacek
4 and Tommy Lee Jones, the film mostly avoids the sudsy atmosphere common to many
5 showbiz tales and emerges as both a wonderful love story and convincing portrayal of one
6 woman's life. As such, the Universal release is in store for some healthy, long-lasting box
7 office action that should reach beyond the realm of country music fans.
8   Lensed on location in Kentucky and Tennessee, Ralf D. Bode's camera effectively
9 utilizes the scenic surroundings as it picks up on thirteen-year-old Spacek and her life in
10 Butcher Hollow. Her parents and five brothers and sisters live in a crowded, broken-down
11 shack; she shoulders much of the responsibility for caring for her siblings; and her future
12 appears to hold only the problems and very occasional joys of those who have lived in the
13 mining town before her.
14   Difference for Spacek, illustrated almost from the beginning, is her attraction to
15 Jones, a magnetic local boy just back from the armed forces who takes a liking to the
16 adolescent. Rising above the depressing atmosphere, the pair generate irresistible roman-
17 tic sparks, whether it be in frequent sarcastic dialogs or an occasional meeting of the eyes.
18 Jones is Spacek's ticket to love and a better life, and despite her youth she is allowed to
19 marry and eventually leave town with her new husband.
20   Film then begins its second section, with more mature Spacek (of 19), the head of her
21 own house with a brood of children. Constantly pushing his wife to improve herself, Jones
22 recognized Spacek's musical talent and buys her a guitar. In short order he has her
23 successfully performing at a local honky-tonk and soon decides to hit out on the road and
24 make his wife a singing star.
25   Rest of picture takes on more of a rags to riches tone as Spacek begins to charm almost
26 everyone across the country with her music and finds, once at the top of the heap, that the
27 pressure puts a crimp in her personal happiness.
28   Director Michael Apted has a lot of ground to cover here but despite film's 125-
29 minute length, he has competently kept the action going. There is seldom a slow moment
30 in the picture, although towards the end short shrift is given to Spacek's bout with drugs,
31 nervous breakdown, marriage troubles, and death of her best friend, Beverly D'Angelo,
32 who turns in a stellar, if abbreviated, performance as country singer Patsy Cline.

33 Spacek also gets fine support from Phyllis Boyens and Levon Helm as her long-
34 suffering parents, latter tearfully accurate as the proverbial poor but decent working man.
35 Tom Rickman has honestly adapted Lynn's autobiography, which she <u>penned</u> with
36 the help of George Vescey. Only <u>drawback</u> is there seems to be some pulling of punches,
37 especially when Lynn's life takes a turn for the worse.
38 Still, Spacek's on-target capturing of the Lynn character is so powerful and pervasive
39 that it picks up any <u>sagging</u> moments in the script. Ditto Jones as her husband, whose
40 <u>ornery</u> <u>nuances</u> don't conceal the fact that in the final analysis he places Spacek above all
41 else.
42 Both Spacek and D'Angelo deserve a special nod of credit for doing all of their own
43 singing with style and accuracy. Although Cline's career is now a memory, Loretta Lynn is
44 still very much a factor in the country music world. That Spacek manages to get inside the
45 Lynn character so completely is what makes "Coal Miner's Daughter" a film that audiences
46 will probably find irresistible.

Reading for Full Comprehension

1. According to the review, who were the cinematographer, the director, and the screenwriter of "Coal Miner's Daughter"?

2. According to this review, what kinds of people will "Coal Miner's Daughter" appeal to?

3. The reviewer believes the film is unrealistic in one respect. What is that?

4. Like the first reviewer, the reviewer divides the film into sections. Where does the second reviewer divide the film? How is this division different from that of the first reviewer?

5. Whose acting in this review is most highly praised?

6. On lines 30–31, the reviewer expresses an opinion about part of the movie. How is that opinion different from or the same as that of the first reviewer?

7. Why does the reviewer feel Spacek and D'Angelo deserve special recognition for their parts?

8. According to this reviewer, who, besides the singer herself, is most responsible for Loretta Lynn's success?

9. There are ten paragraphs in this review. Place the numbers of the correct paragraphs after each question.

   A. Which paragraph describes the pace of the movie?

   B. Which paragraph summarizes the author's opinion of the performance of the two main characters?

   C. Which four paragraphs summarize the action of the movie?

10. Summarize this reading selection in 75 to 100 words.

WRITING ASSIGNMENTS

1. Write a paper, based on the first three articles, in which you trace the impact of modernization on Appalachia from the time of the Civil War to the present. Write summaries of the three articles to show what modernization took place and then describe how it impacted the region.

2. Write a short paper on one or two social problems in Appalachia. Describe the problems, show their causes, and their solutions.

3. Compare and contrast the two film reviews. Write a paragraph summarizing one, and a second paragraph summarizing the other and comparing/contrasting it to the first.

4. Consider the American definition of progress given in the first article. Examine some of the ways *this definition* has affected America's relations with your country. Limit yourself to those areas that can be described within the context of this definition.

5. Is there an area such as Appalachia in your country? If there is, compare/contrast two or three of the regional features of the two areas.

6. In the first article, the author makes two points: that Americans believe in progress and that Americans tend to equate progress with modernization. Based on what you have learned in this chapter, do you believe Americans are justified in continuing to believe in modernization as a force of progress? State your opinion in a clear thesis, and, with reference to information in the chapter, support your position in three or four paragraphs.

7. Write a letter to friends in your country in which you suggest that they go see (not go see) the movie. Then, explain your reasons for your opinion in two or three paragraphs.

USING LIBRARY INDEXES

You may want to learn more about one of the films or one of the related issues discussed in this text. The following information is presented to assist you in using reference indexes you will need to access in order to locate information on related subjects or films.

A library consists of three sections: reference, stacks, and circulation. In the reference section, you will find indexes that can help you locate material in the stacks, material that you can then take to the circulation desk to check out. Indexes, usually bound in annual volumes, are particularly useful because they provide citations to newspaper, magazine, journal, and periodical articles that have been written on every conceivable subject. Indexes, however, are generally specialized, that is they index material from a specific type of publication. For example, the *Humanities Index* has material from over three hundred journals and magazines that are concerned with such subjects as history, literature, the classics, art, language, and linguistics. The *Social Science Index* covers material from over three hundred journals and periodicals that contain articles in the social sciences. The *Alternative Press Index: An Index to Alternative and Radical Publications* includes material from over two hundred publications that are considered alternative or radical. Publications espousing a particular lifestyle, political philosophy, or environmental perspective are often indexed in the *Alternative Press Index*. These are just three of the many specialized indexes available to you in the reference section of most libraries.

These indexes, although very useful, should not necessarily be your first choice when selecting an index. The *Reader's Guide to Periodical Literature*, an index to general journals and periodicals, is often the best to begin with as you start to research a topic. The *Reader's Guide* indexes material from such publications as *Newsweek, Time, Reader's Digest, the New Yorker*, and *U.S. News & World Report*, and, like specialized indexes, it lists citations by alphabetical subject and subheadings. The following example is taken from the *Reader's Guide to Periodical Literature*:

MINORITIES
        See also
    Discrimination
    Intelligence—Minorities
Bon temps minority [bill passed designating Cajuns as a
    minority group] il *Time* 131:32 Je 13 '88

The demography of a dream. H. Cisneros, il *New Perspectives*
    Quarterly 5:36–9 Summ '88

Civil Rights

See also
United Nations, Subcommission on Prevention of
    Discrimination and Protection of Minorities.

Crime

See also
Ethnic gangs & organized crime [*cover story; special section*]
    il *U.S. News & World Report* 104:29–31+ Ja 18 '88

Education

See also
Bilingual education
Institute for Independent Education
Playing to Win (Organization)
Public schools—Desegregation
SHARP Program
The Berkeley squeeze [effects of affirmative action]
    J. S. Gibney. *The New Republic* 198:15–17 Ap 11 '88
Canon fodder [changing the Great Books requirement to meet
    minority demands at Stanford University] N. Glazer. *The
    New Republic* 199:19–21 Ag. 22 '88
The crisis of minorities in higher education [address,
    February 12, 1988] R. Wilson. *Vital Speeches of the Day*
    54:473–6 My 15 '88
The dismal panorama of urban schools. G. I. Maeroff. *The
    Education Digest* 54:7–10 S '88
Educating more minority engineers. E. W. Gordon, il
    Technology Review 91:68–73 Jl '88
Financial aid and minority access. G. A. Jackson. il
    Change 20:48–9 S/O '88
Give them a guarantee [E. Lang pays college tuition for
    Harlem students] M. Magnet. *The Washington Monthly*
    20:31–2 Je '88

Notice that under the subject heading "MINORITIES" there are subheadings "Civil
Rights," "Crime," and "Education" that narrow the subject's focus. Note that the subject
headings, like the subheadings, are listed in alphabetical order and often contain "see
also" sections that suggest alternative subject headings. Unlike the subheadings, subject
headings are written entirely in capitals and are placed at the margins. A subheading's
first letter is capitalized and it is centered, not placed at the margin. Also note what
information is usually found in an individual citation: the title, the author's name (the
author's first name is represented by an initial), the publications's name (written in
italicized script), a volume number (followed by a colon), the page numbers the article

can be found on, and the date of the publication. In the following example, under the subject heading "ASIAN AMERICANS" and the subheading "Crimes against," the article entitled "Scapegoats Again" was written by M. Moore and includes an illustration. (The abbreviation "il" between "M. Moore" and *"The Progressive"* indicates there is an illustration with the article.) Additionally, the article was published in *The Progressive* in volume 52 on pages 25 through 27 in the fall edition of 1988.

ASIAN AMERICANS

America's new talent bank. D. Gergen, il *U.S. News & World Report* 104:80 Mr 14 '88

The Asian-American success myth. C. Peacock. il *Utne Reader* p22–3 Mr/Ap '88

The 'eastern capital' of Asia. J. Schwartz. il *Newsweek* 111:56–8 F 22 '88

How three groups overcame prejudice. I. Peck il *Scholastic Update* (Teacher's edition) 120:12–13 My 6 '88

Crimes against

Scapegoats again. M. Moore. il *The Progressive* 52:25–7 F '88

Education

See also

Asian American college students

Are Asian-American kids really smarter? B. Diamond. il *Seventeen* 47:176–7 + My '88

The model minority goes to school. D. Divoky. bibl f il *Phi Delta Kappan* 70:219–22 N '88

On campus, stereotypes persist [quotas for admission] A. Levine, il *U.S. News & World Report* 104:53 Mr 28 '88

Working effectively with Asian immigrant parents. E. L. Yao. bibl f il *Phi Delta Kappan* 70:223–5 N '88

Political Activities

Growing pains [Monterey Park, Calif.] N. Lemann. il *The Atlantic* 261:56–62 Ja '88

Newspaper indexes are other useful indexes. Most major American newspapers are indexed. Like the periodical indexes, citations are indexed alphabetically according to subject matter, and, like periodical indexes, newspaper indexes are published in annual volumes. *The Christian Science Monitor Index, The Chicago Tribune Index, The New York Times Index, The Los Angeles Times Index,* and *The Official Washington Post Index* are all useful sources for discovering information contained in these newspapers.

Being able to select an appropriate index and read a citation is useless unless you are able to first locate the appropriate subject heading. A useful strategy to employ when trying to think of an appropriate subject heading is to look under the most general word that you can think of that describes the subject on which you are interested in locating information. For example, if after viewing the film *Stand and Deliver*, you decide to do research on discrimination in education, first look up the word "EDUCATION." Under the subject heading "EDUCATION," you will notice that in addition to the subheadings there is also a section called "see also." The words contained in both the subheadings and the "see also" section should allow you to narrow the focus of your search.

However, if after you have thought of a general word you still don't discover a subject heading, you may need to think of synonyms for the word you have selected, or expand or narrow your search. For example, if you look under "DISCRIMINATION" and don't find anything, you may want to look under a synonym for "DISCRIMINATION," such as "RACISM" or "PREJUDICE." If after choosing several synonyms you are still unable to locate a subject heading, you may want to expand your search. For example, if after watching *Coal Miner's Daughter*, you decide you want to learn more about honky-tonk music, you may want to look under a more general heading such as "COUNTRY MUSIC." Or, if after watching *Dim Sum* you are interested in learning more about Asian Americans, and look under "ASIANS," you will find that it is too general. You will need to narrow your search to "ASIAN AMERICANS." Generally, if you are able to think of one appropriate subject heading, you will be able to narrow your subject by examining the "see also" section and the subheadings under the subject heading. If not, expand or narrow your search.

If your purpose is to locate an additional review you can use any one of the previously mentioned indexes. In order to locate a film review in one of those indexes, you should look under one of the following subject headings: "MOTION PICTURE REVIEWS" or "FILM REVIEW," the title of the movie, or the director's name. However, before doing that, you will need to know when the film was released, since most films are reviewed around the same time they are released. If you want to find a review of a film released in 1980, it is not advisable to use the 1987 *Reader's Guide to Periodical Literature*.

In addition to using the previously mentioned indexes to locate a film review, you can consult specialized film indexes. *Variety Film Reviews*, published on an annual basis, contains all the reviews published in *Variety*, a motion-picture industry publication. This reference book contains the actual review, not a citation of the review. In order to use *Variety Film Reviews*, you will need to know when the film was released, since the films are listed according to when they were released. Volumes 1, 2, and 3, of the *Index to Critical Film Review* are also useful; however, it cites films only up until 1976. It is arranged in alphabetical order according to the title of the film. Under the title of each film is a list of citations on reviews of the film. The *Film Review Index*, volumes 1 and 2, is an excellent source for finding film reviews, although it only cites films released before 1986. In it you will find films listed in alphabetical order according to title. Under each title is production information on the film (e.g., who produced, directed, wrote, filmed, and starred in the film) and a listing of film review citations. *Magills Cinema Annual*, published yearly, also contains a listing of film reviews for a selected number of film titles arranged in alphabetical order. In addition, a synopsis of each film is included. *Film Review Annual*, published yearly since 1981, contains at least one selected review on each film indexed and for many films six or seven reviews. Additionally, citations on more reviews are also included. Films are listed by title in the *Film Review Annual*.

Whether you choose a general index such as the *Reader's Guide to Periodical Literature* or a specialized film index such as *Film Review Index*, you will notice that certain publications are frequently cited as containing film reviews. They include the following: *Time, Newsweek, Christian Science Monitor,* the *New York Times, Newsday,* and *New Republic.* If you are looking for reviews in these publications they are most often found under sections called "The Arts" or "Entertainment." However, if a film is already on video, it is difficult to just thumb through these periodicals to find a review. Thumbing through these publications might be useful for locating a review of a film currently playing in theaters. However, to find a review for a film on video, you will need to go to one of the indexes mentioned in this chapter to discover where you can locate a review.

Once you have located several citations, whether they be for reviews or for information on a related subject, you need to discover whether your library carries the publication that is cited. That information will be on microfiche, computer, and/or a serial record. (A serial record is a listing of all serials the library subscribes to, as the card catalog is a listing of all books the library has purchased.) For instance, if the citation indicates the review or article you want to find is in the magazine *The New Yorker* and is contained in volume 1, you need to find out from the microfilm record, the library's computer record, or the serial record whether the library subscribes to *The New Yorker,* and if it does, whether it keeps back copies. If so, you need to find out whether these back copies go as far back as volume 1. If you find that the answer to each of these questions is yes, it is then that you need to write down the call number of the publication and locate it in the stacks.

The stacks is the part of the library where material, other than reference material, is located. Since most periodicals are bound after they have been circulated for six months to a year in the current periodicals section, it is likely that within a rather large bound volume you will find the article you need. Also, be aware that most newspapers and many magazines are put on microfilm rather than bound. It saves space for the library. When you first find the publication listed on the microfiche, computer, or serial record, it should indicate whether the material is bound and/or on microfilm. If it is on microfilm, you will need to have the library make a copy of the article or you will need to use a microfilm copy machine. If the article is in a bound volume, you will need to check it out at circulation, the third part of the library.

Library circulation sections will often only allow you to have a bound volume of periodicals for a short time (from two hours to two days is typical). So, very often, you will need to photocopy the article from the bound volume.

By using the indexes described in this section, you should be able to find more information on any subject introduced in one of the eight films in this textbook or additional reviews of the films. The following is a listing of the indexes discussed in this chapter presented as a brief summary.

GENERAL PERIODICAL INDEX

1. *Reader's Guide to Periodical Literature*

SPECIALIZED PERIODICAL INDEX

1. *Humanities Index*

2. *Social Science Index*

3. *Alternative Press Index*

NEWSPAPER INDEXES

1. *The Christian Science Monitor*

2. *The Chicago Tribune Index*

3. *The New York Times Index*

4. *The Los Angeles Times Index*

5. *The Official Washington Post Index*

FILM REVIEW INDEXES

1. *The Index to Critical Film Reviews (–1970)*

2. *The Film Review Index (–1985)*

3. *Magills Cinema Annual*

4. *Film Review Annual*

REFERENCE BOOKS THAT CONTAIN ACTUAL REVIEWS

1. *Film Review Annual*

2. *Variety Film Reviews*